Colorful Meditating:
An Adult Coloring Book

Theresa Beebe

ISBN-13: 978-1530313617
ISBN-10: 1530313619

ACKNOWLEDGMENTS

I want to personally thank the following people (in no particular order) for their contributions to my inspiration and knowledge and immense support in creating this book: Maria (my mom), Robert, Steven, Katy, Mark and Kathie, Diane and Evan, Jodi and David, Trysette, Fiona, Franky, Tawni, Tom, and Georganna, Ina, Alice and all who have been and are a part of my life.   You will always have a very special place in my heart.

Special thank you to my daughter, Maria Hayley for her beautiful coloring. Maria, I am so proud of you and proud you are part of this. I look forward to more projects with you.

Also, I want to thank Jennifer for her assistance. You are beautiful and an inspiration.

Thank you for being part of the journey.

Welcome and thank you for buying this book.

These pictures can be colored using colored markers, crayons, colored pencils or other similar media. Depending on the type of media you use, it could bleed through the paper. I recommend using a separate piece of paper underneath to protect the next page.

Feel free to add your own tangles to open spaces in and around the mandalas. You can also use the pictures to practice shading which adds a lot of depth and contour.

Sometimes coming up with different colors can be a challenge. Here are a few websites which have information and guides to help you choose:
   https://coolors.co/
   https://color.adobe.com/create/color-wheel/
   http://www.tigercolor.com/color-lab/color-theory/color-theory-intro.htm

I want to see how you bring them to life. Please send them to me at:
   mytangledjourney@gmail.com.

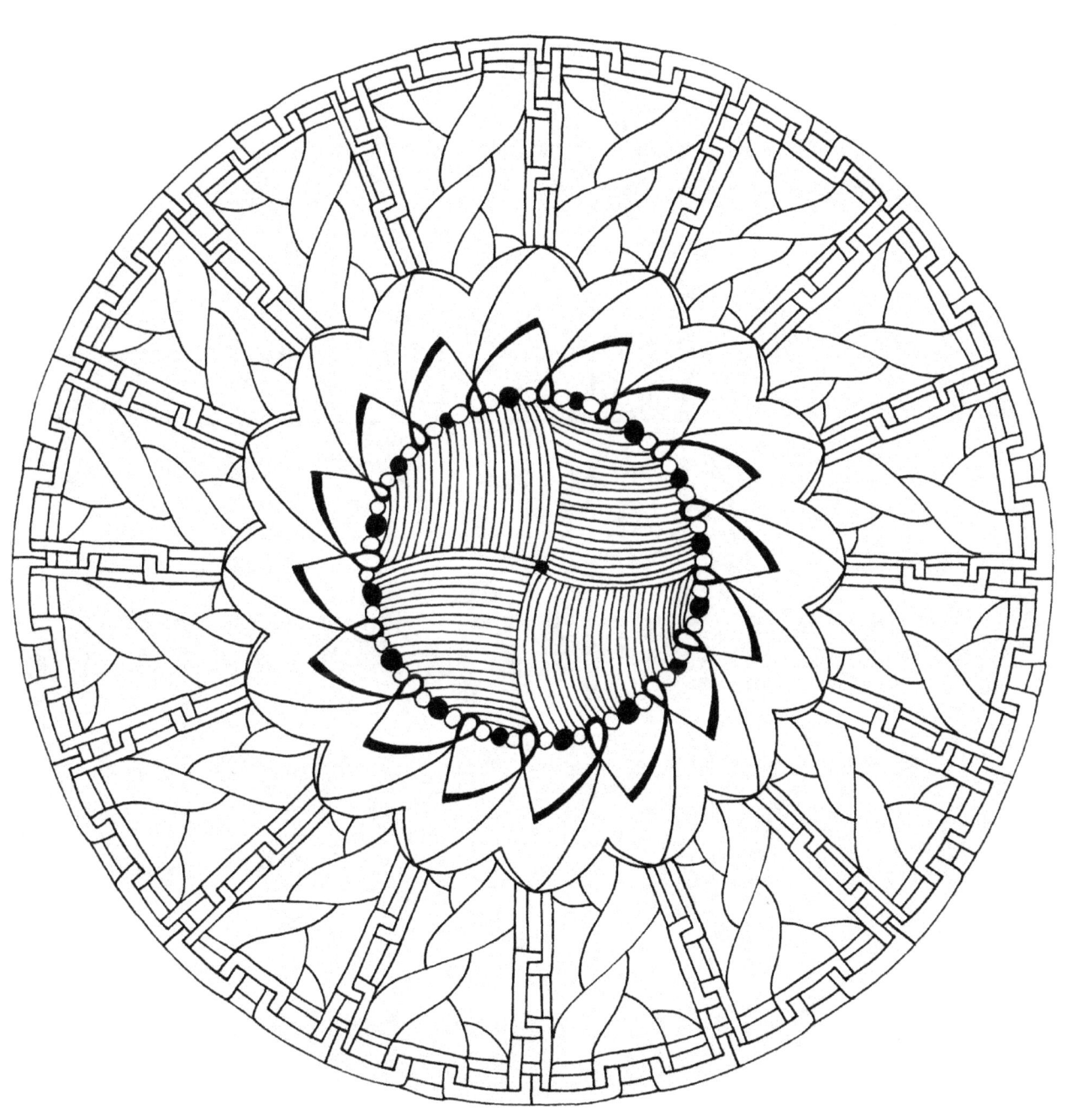

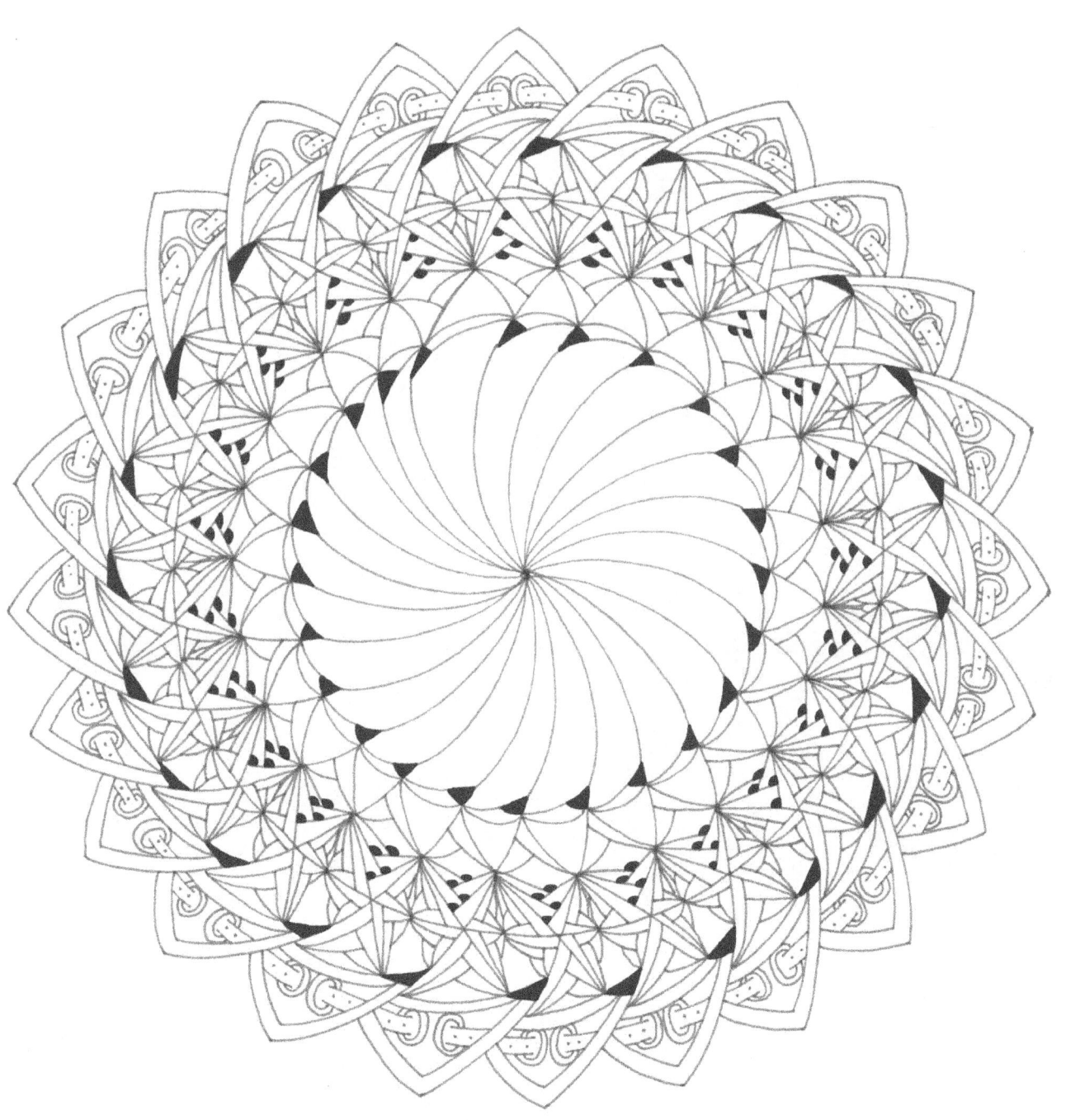

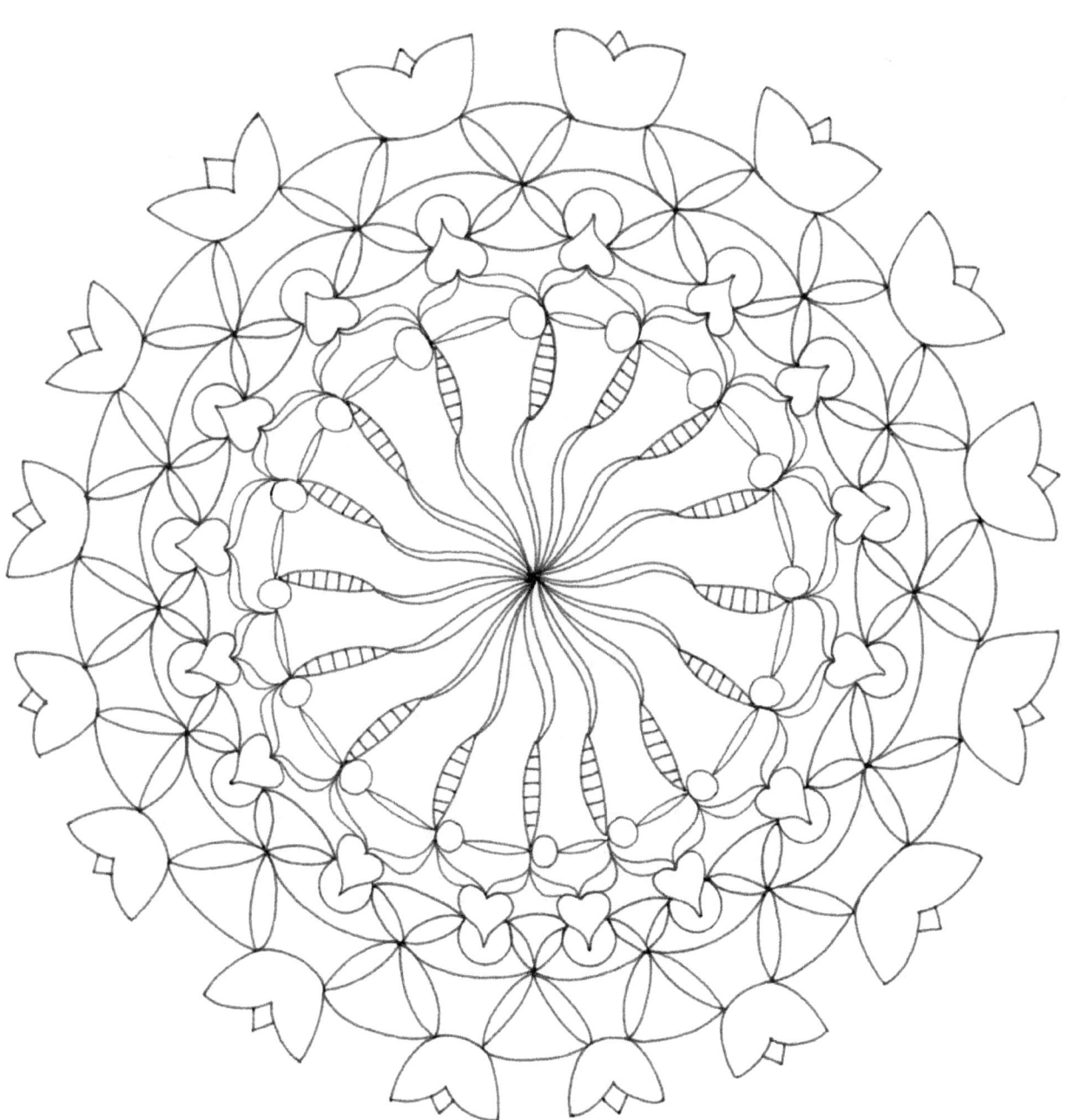

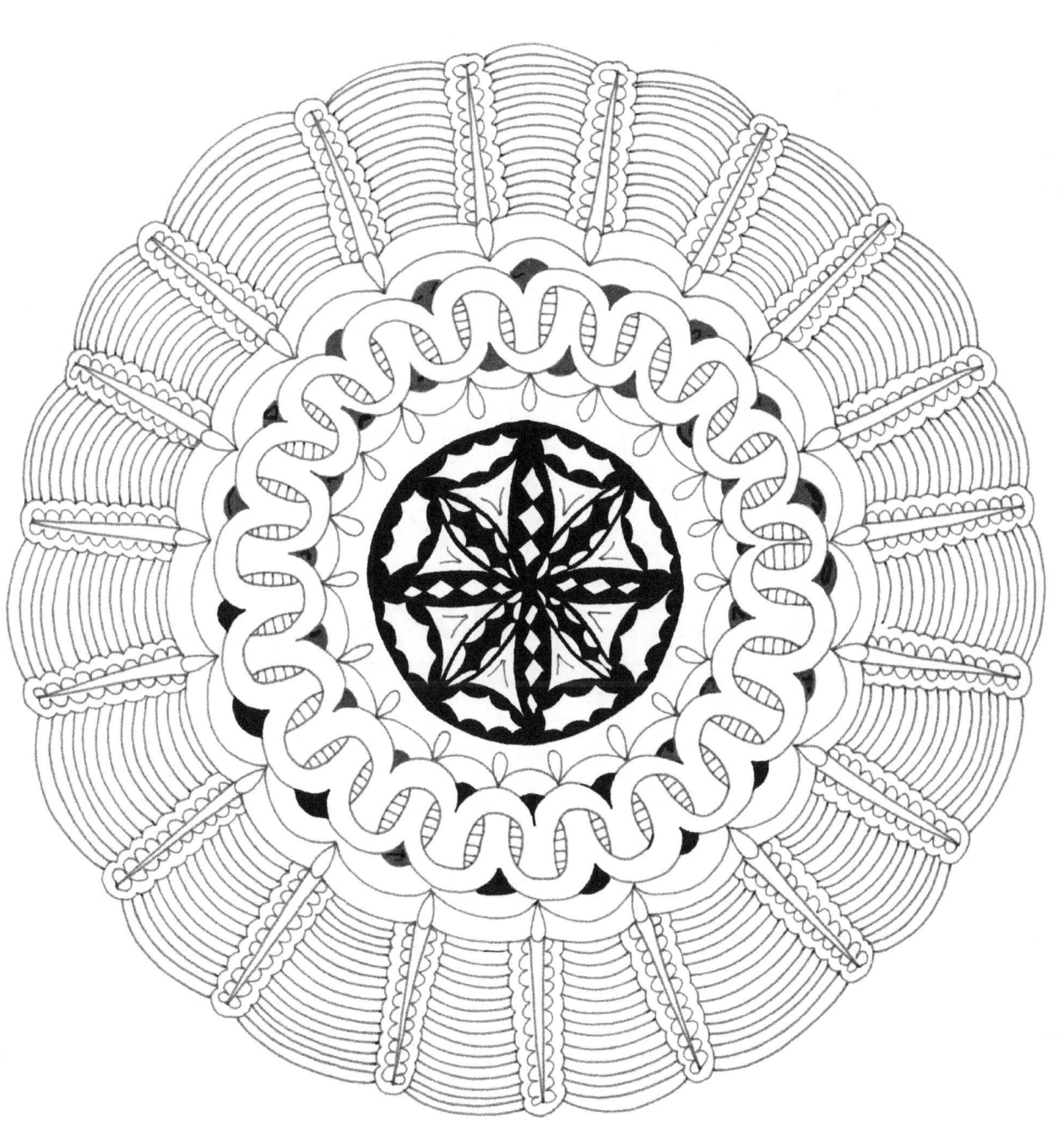

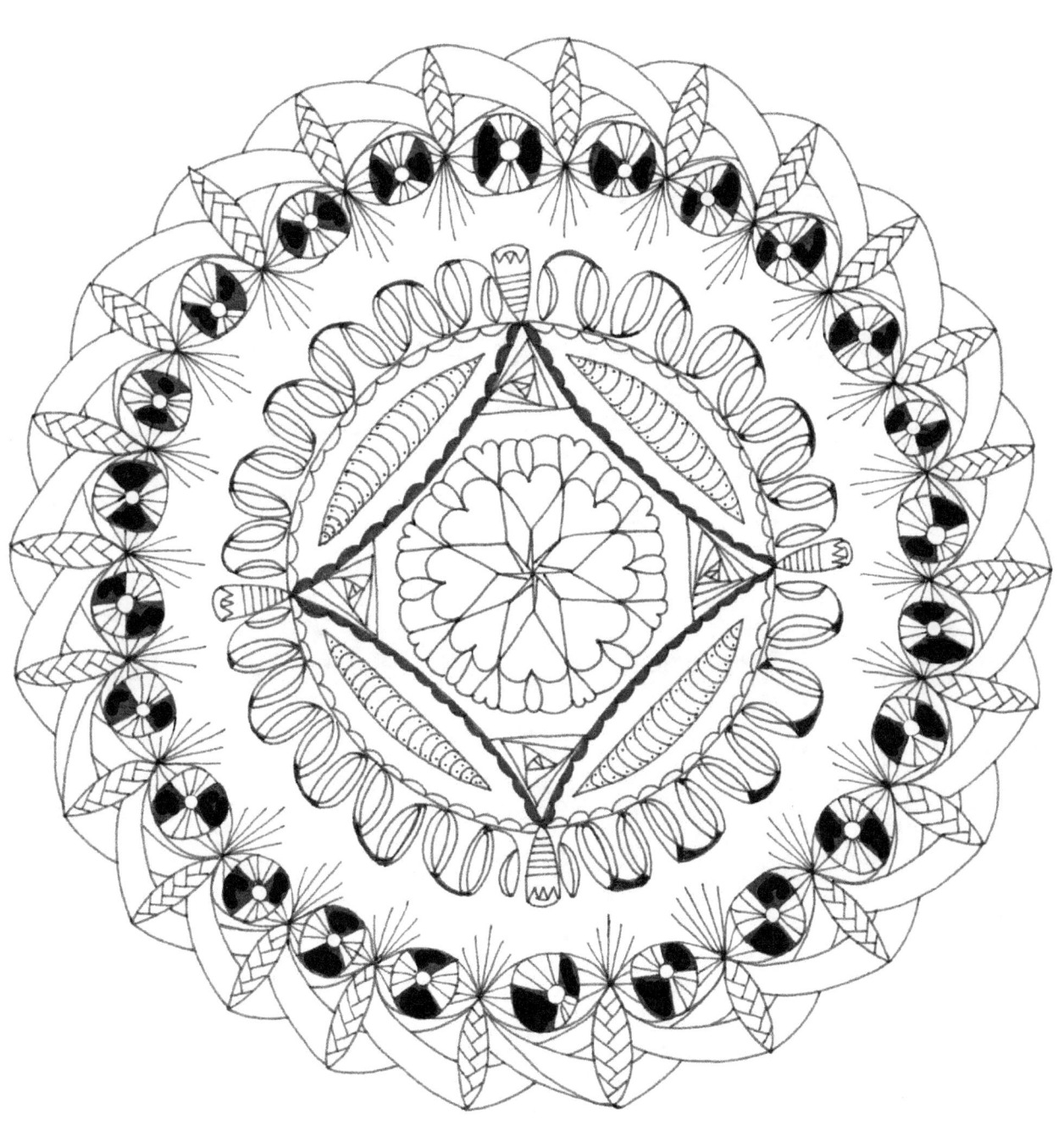

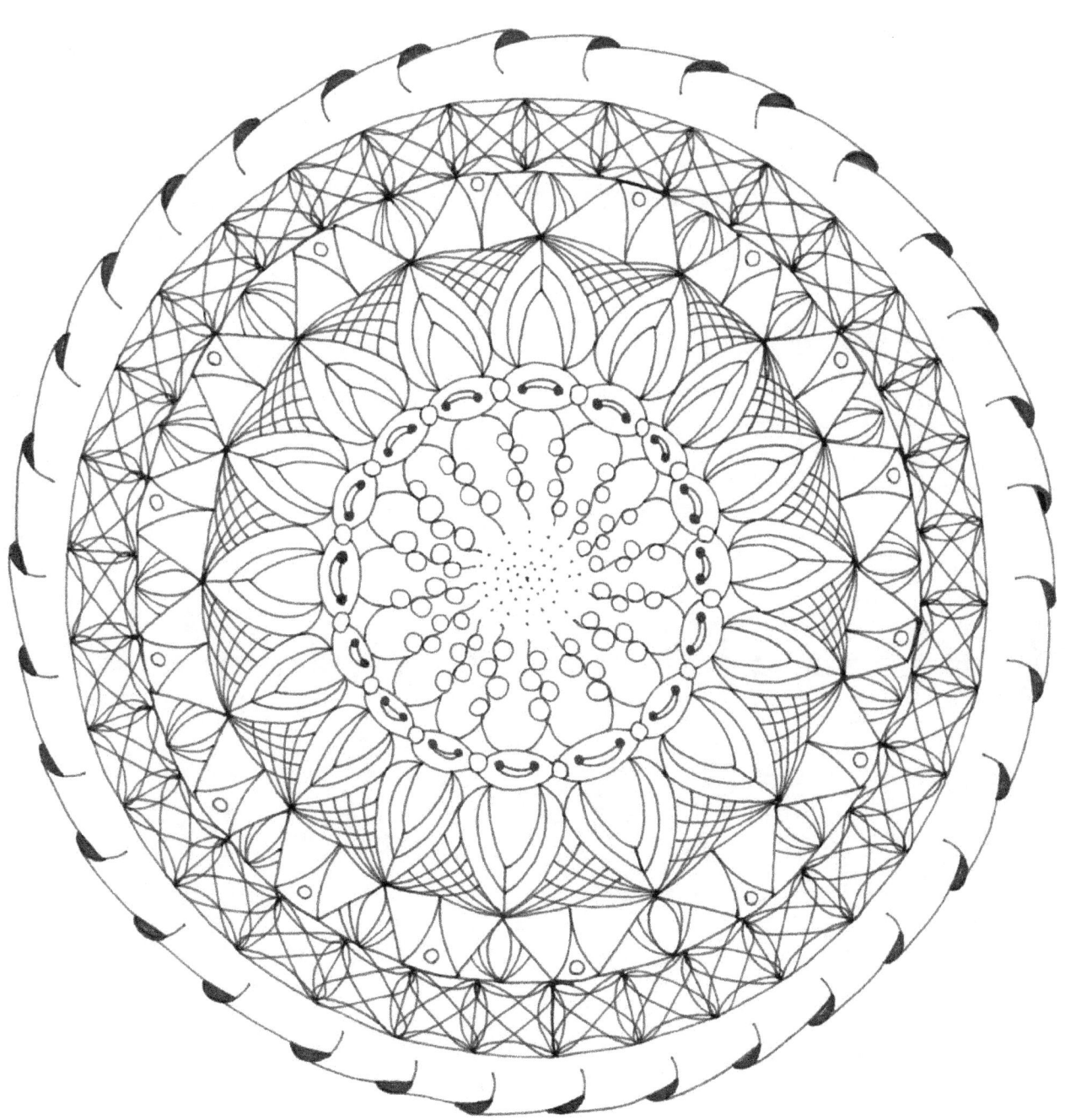

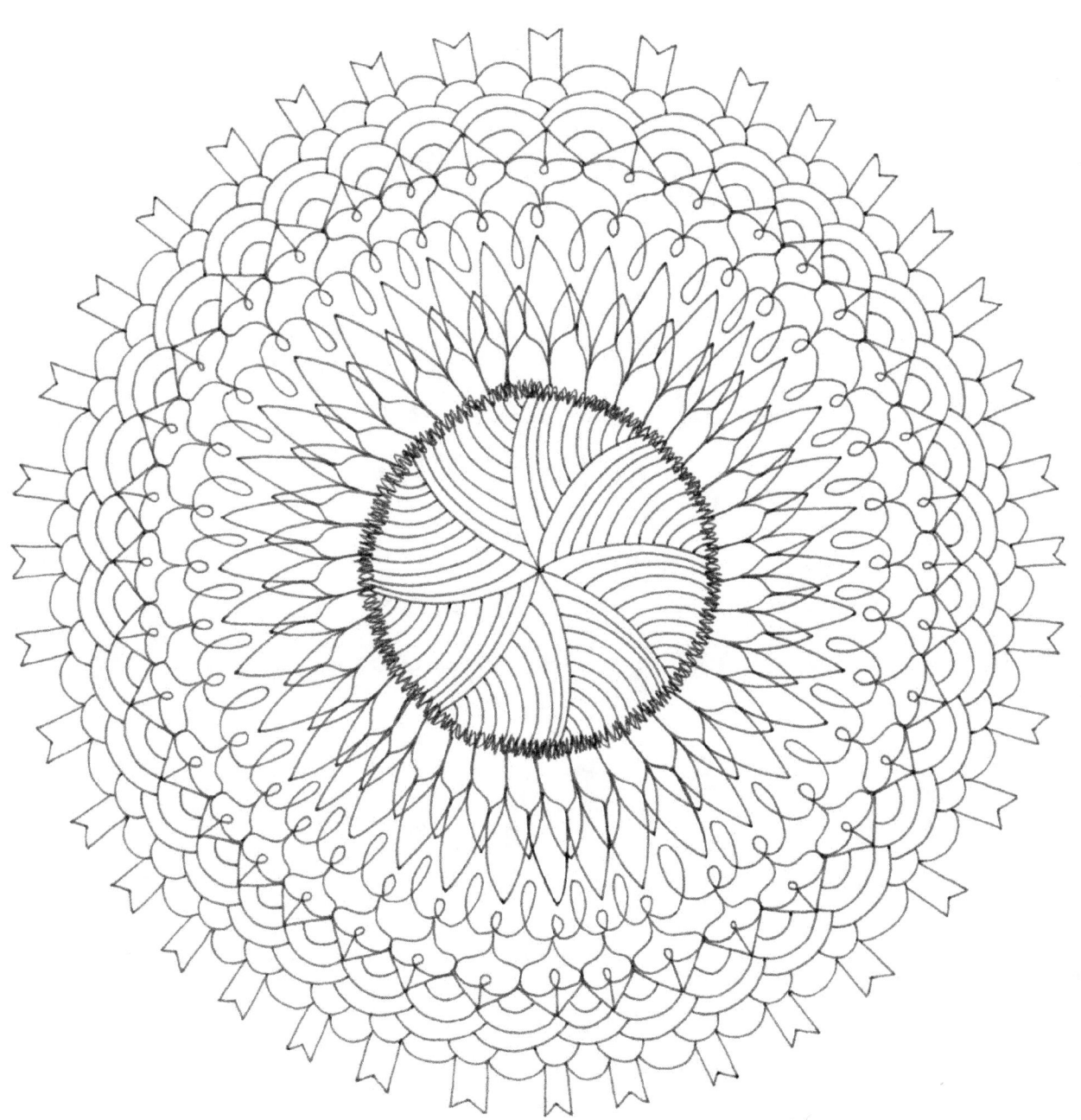

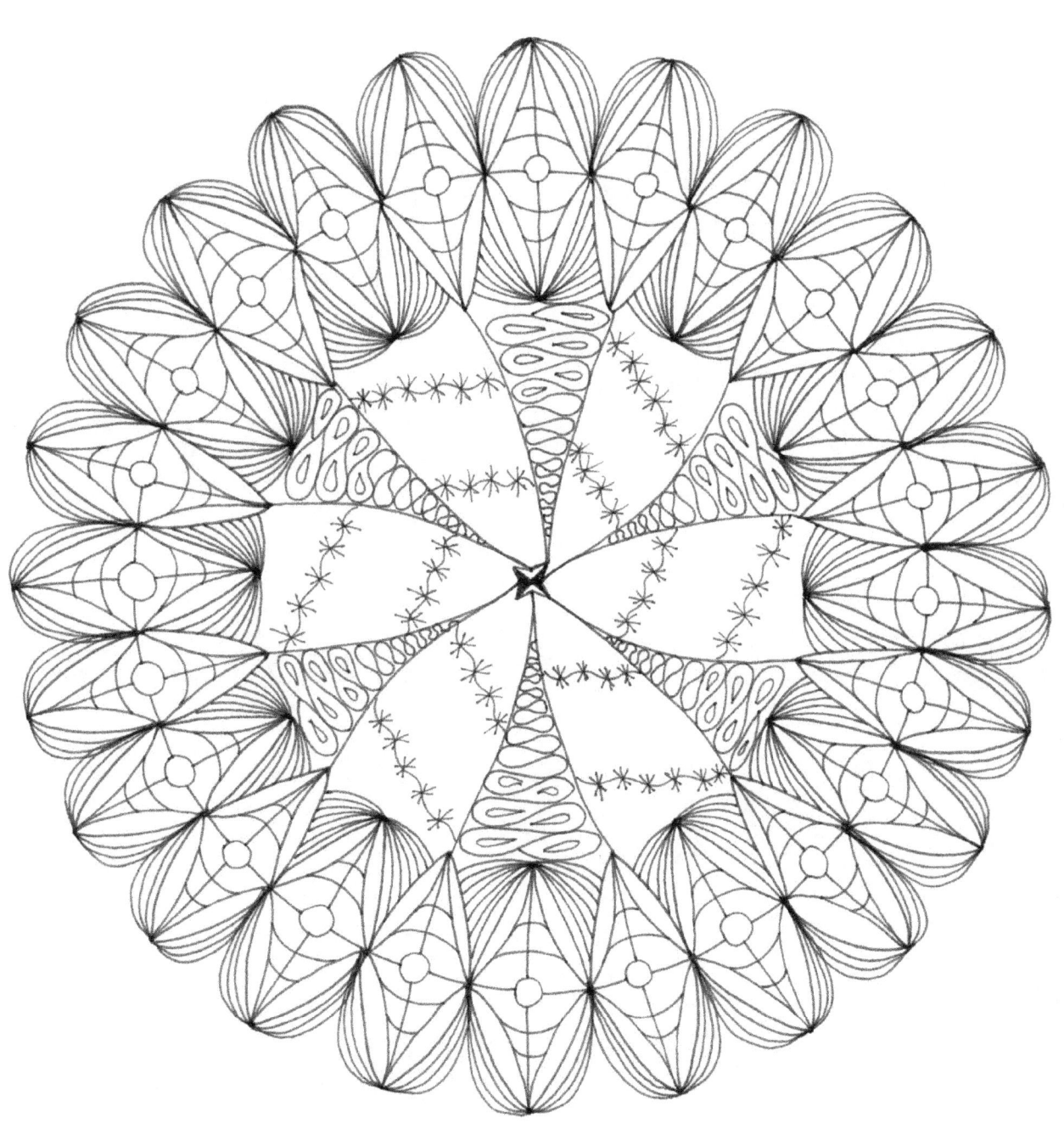

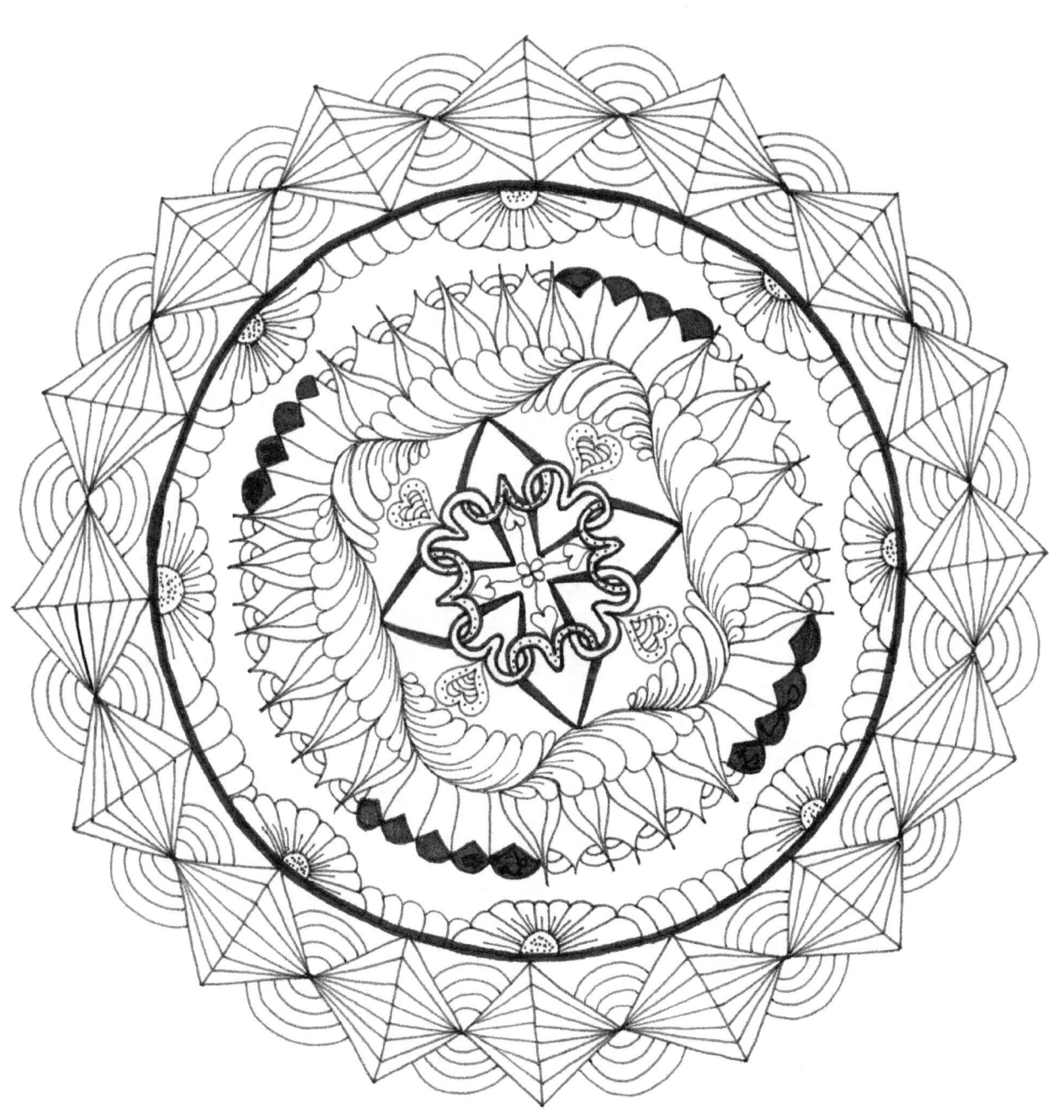

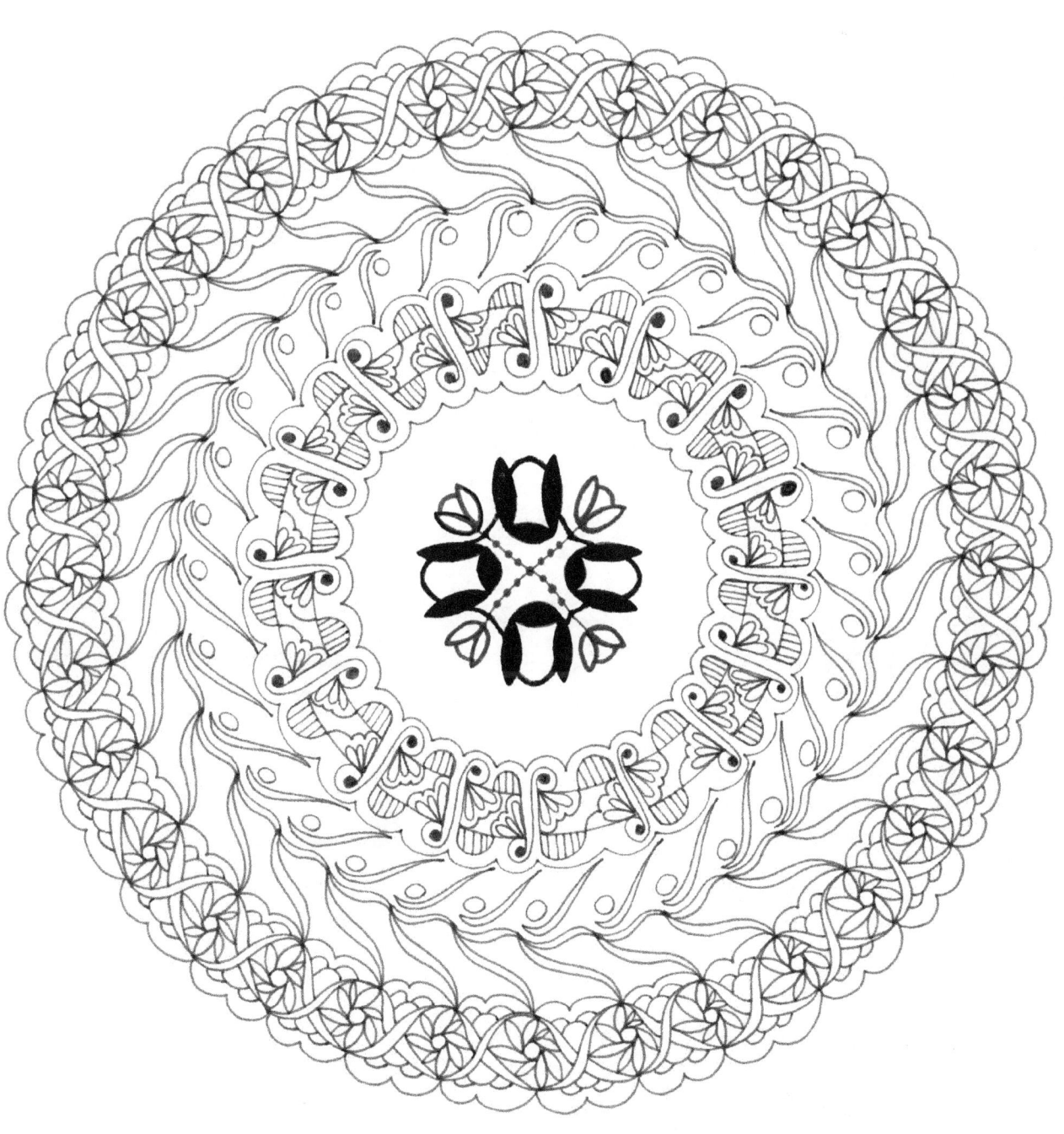

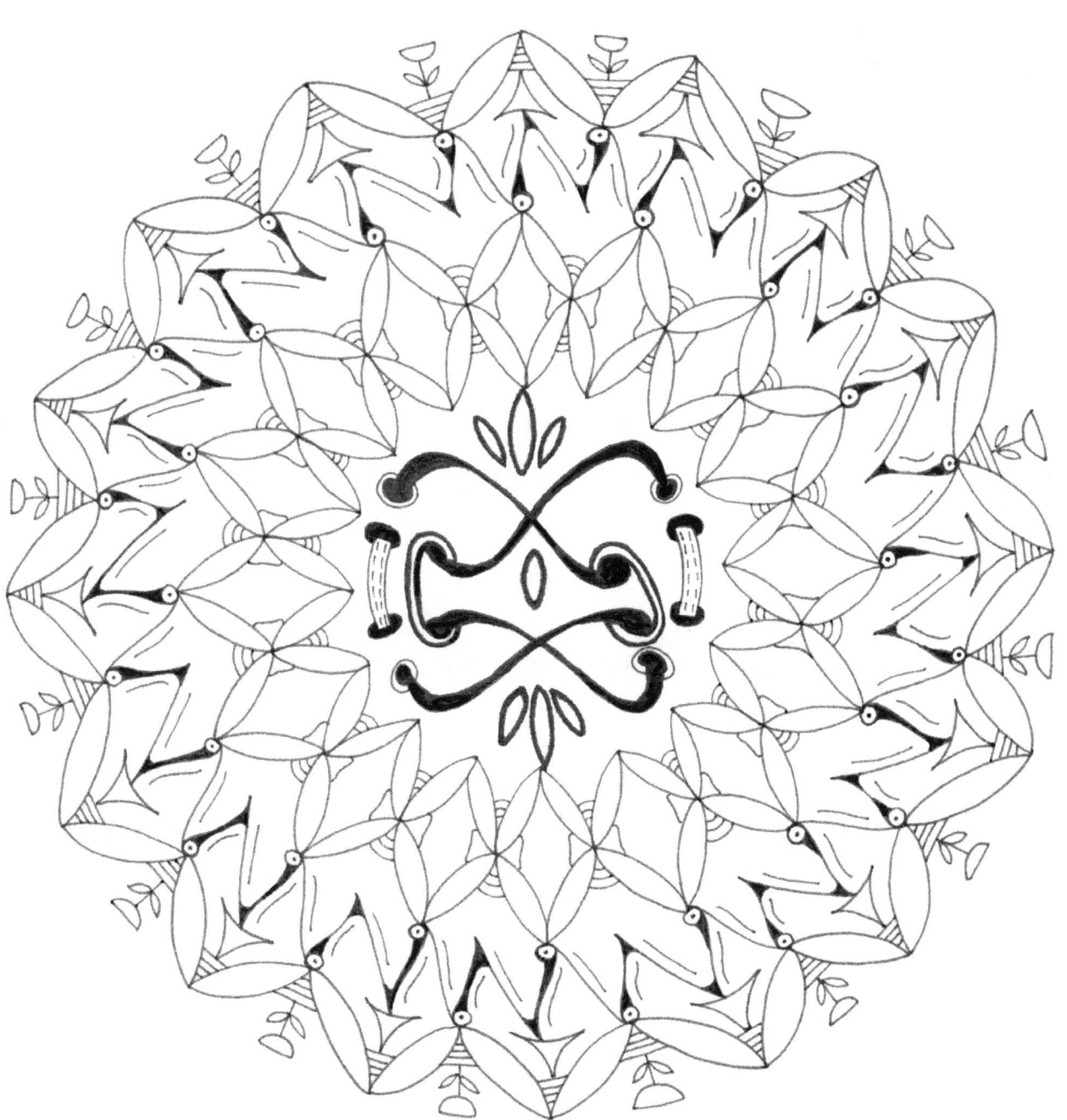

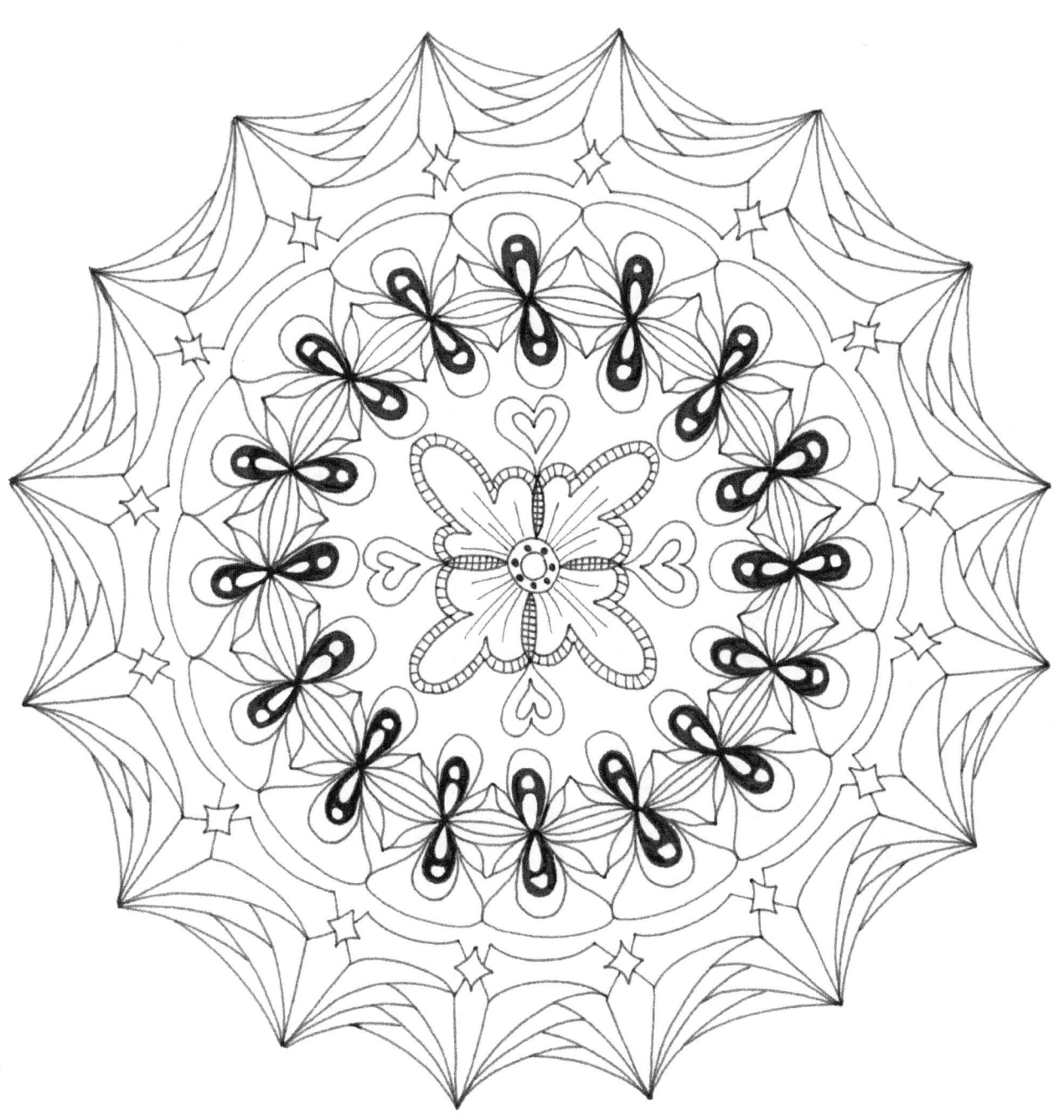

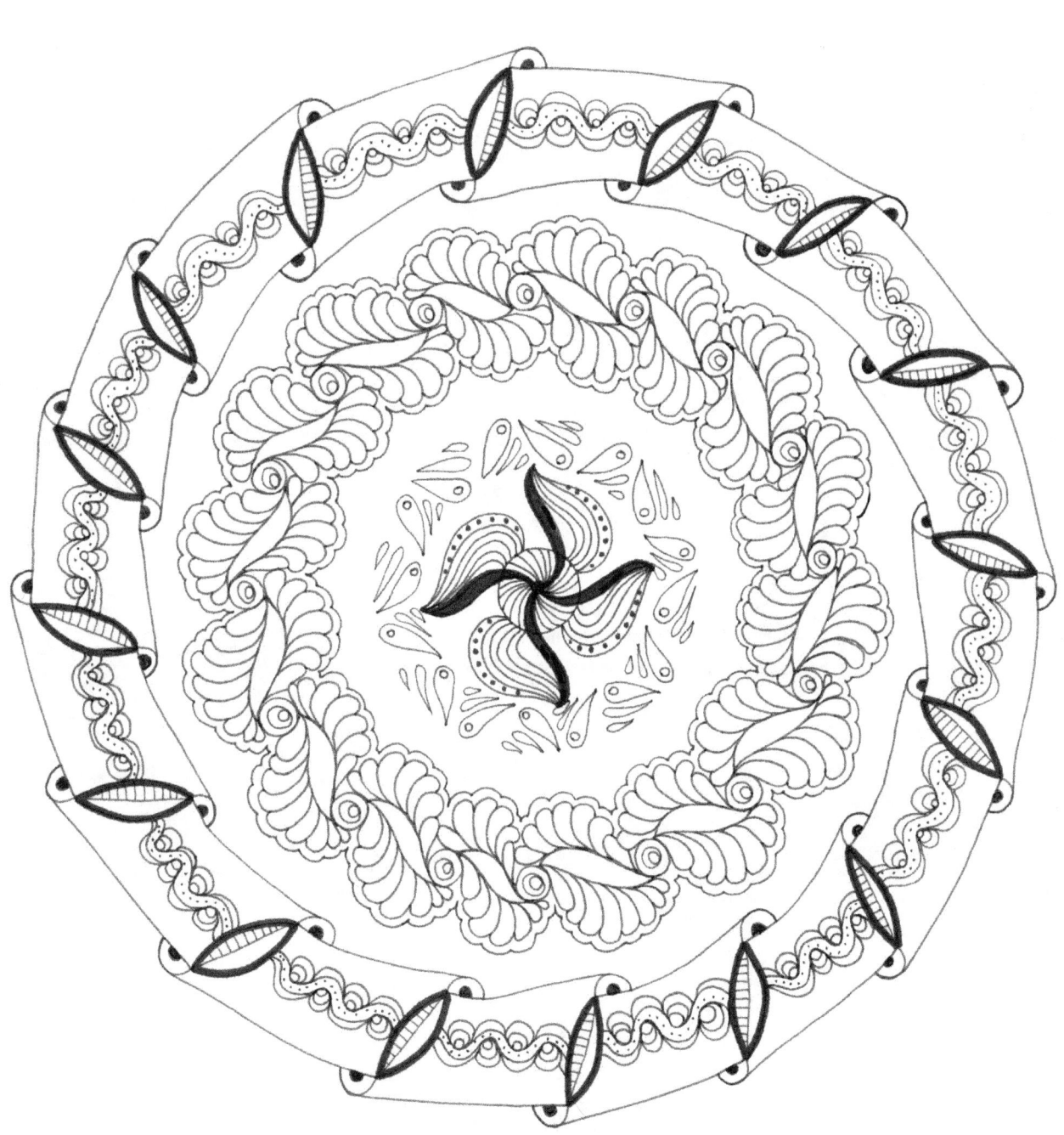

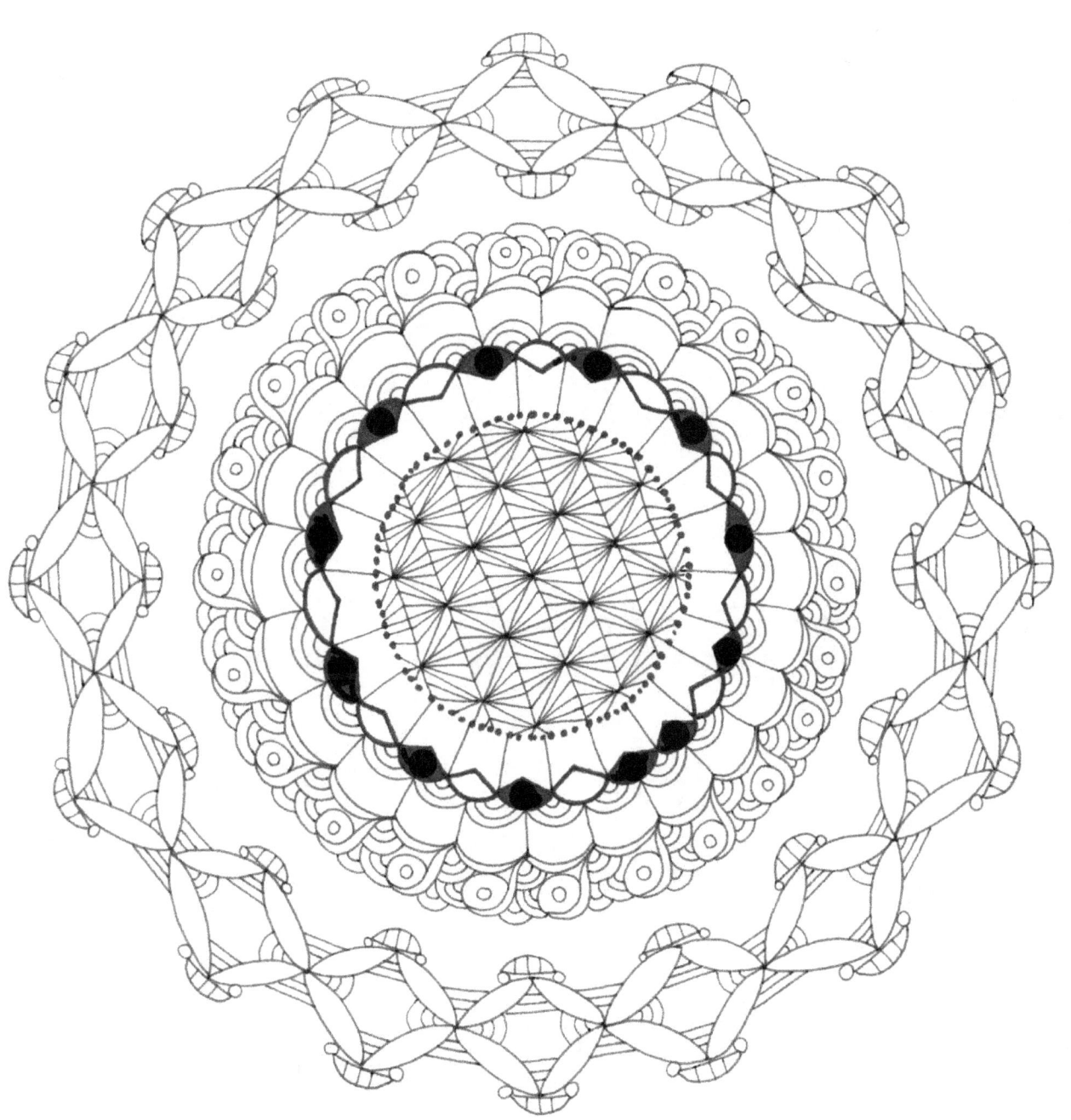

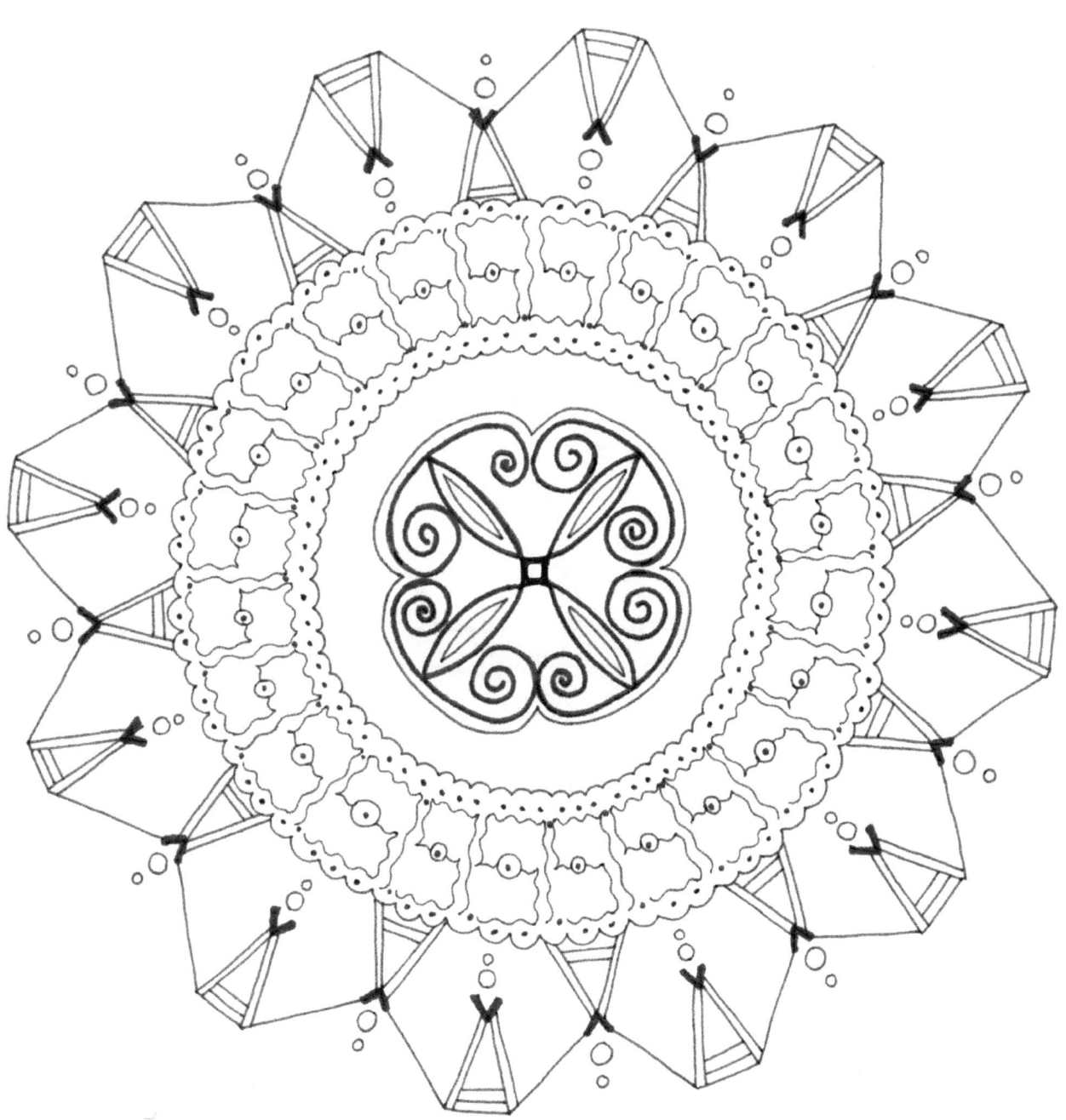

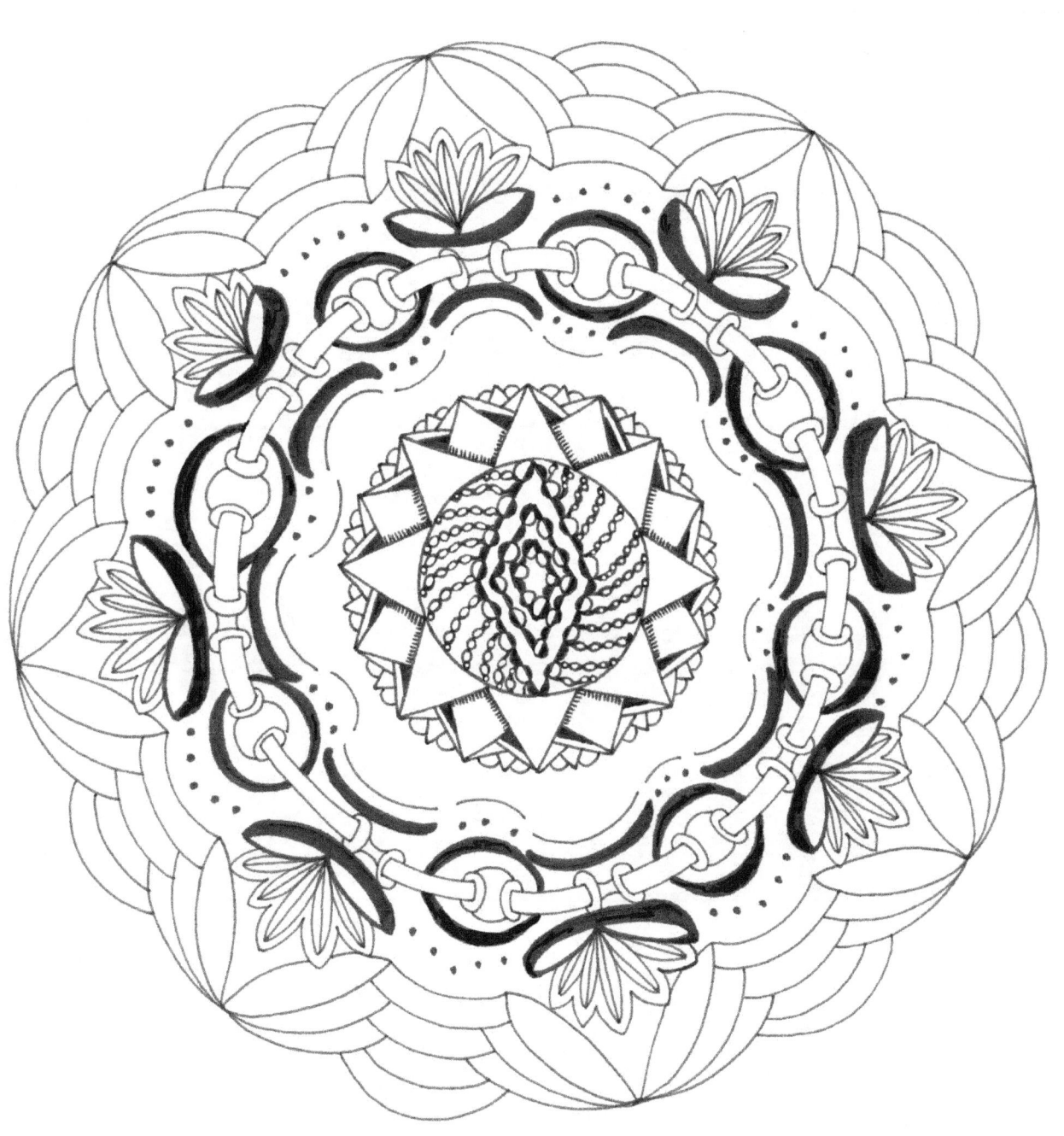

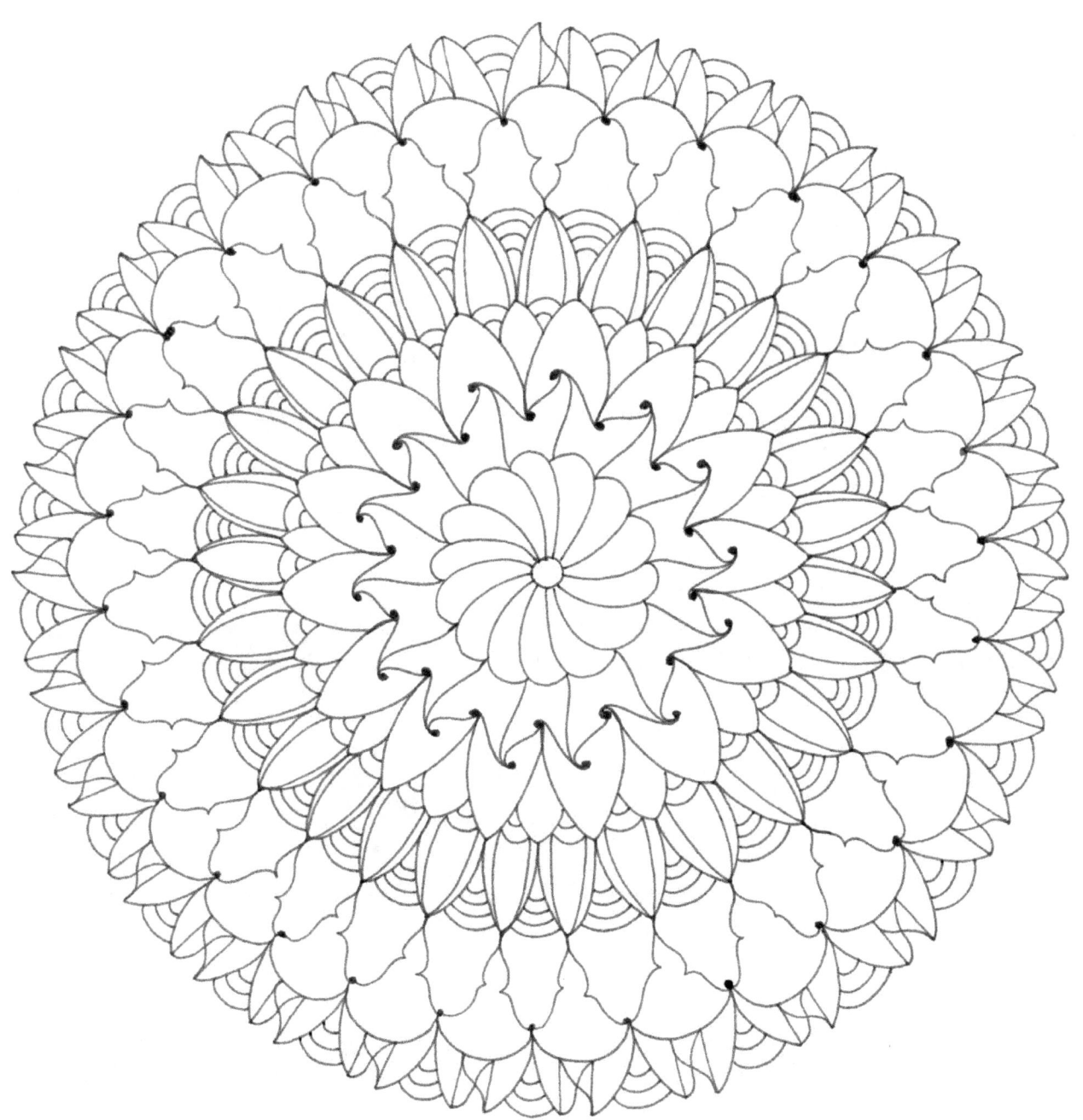

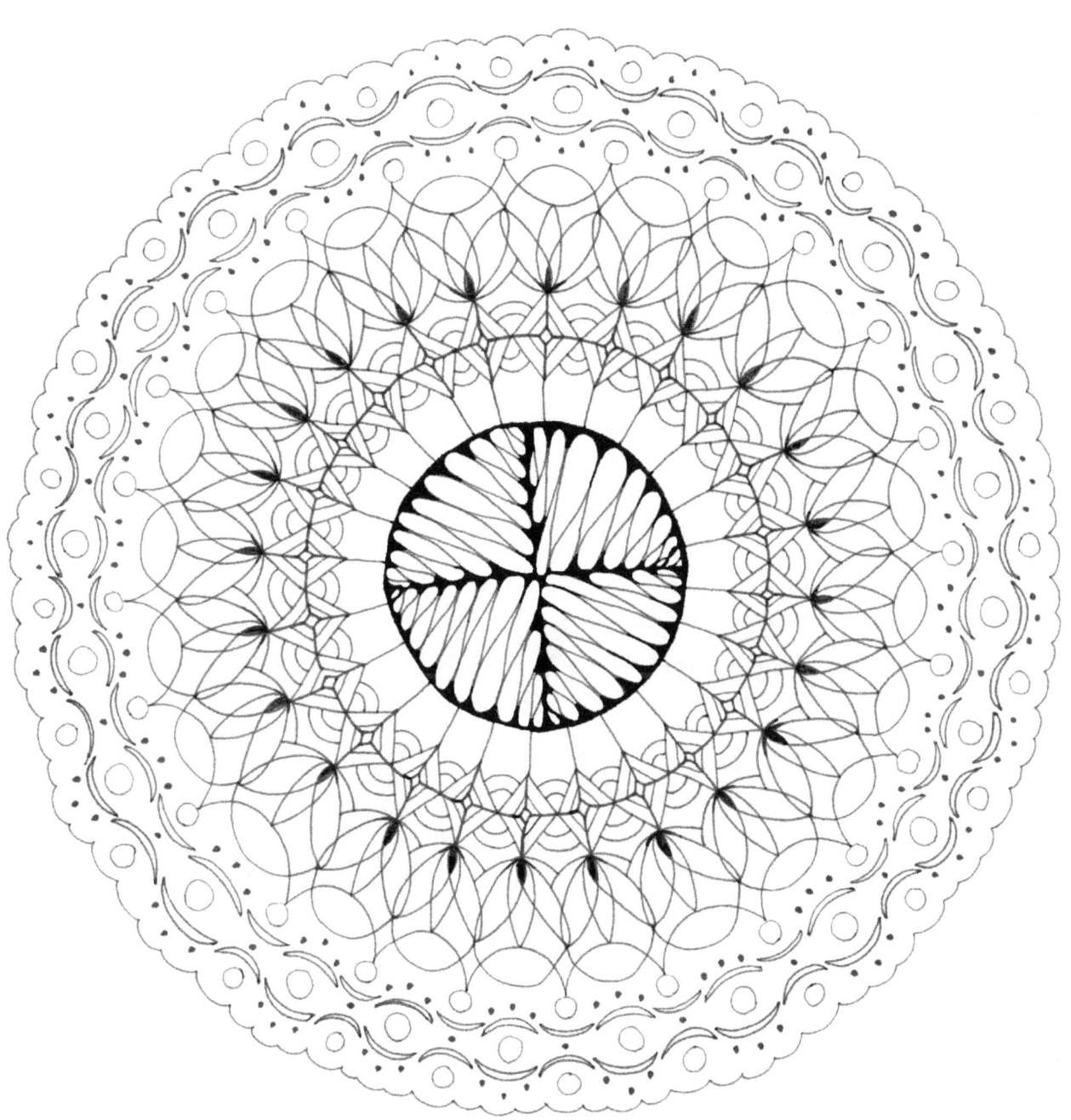

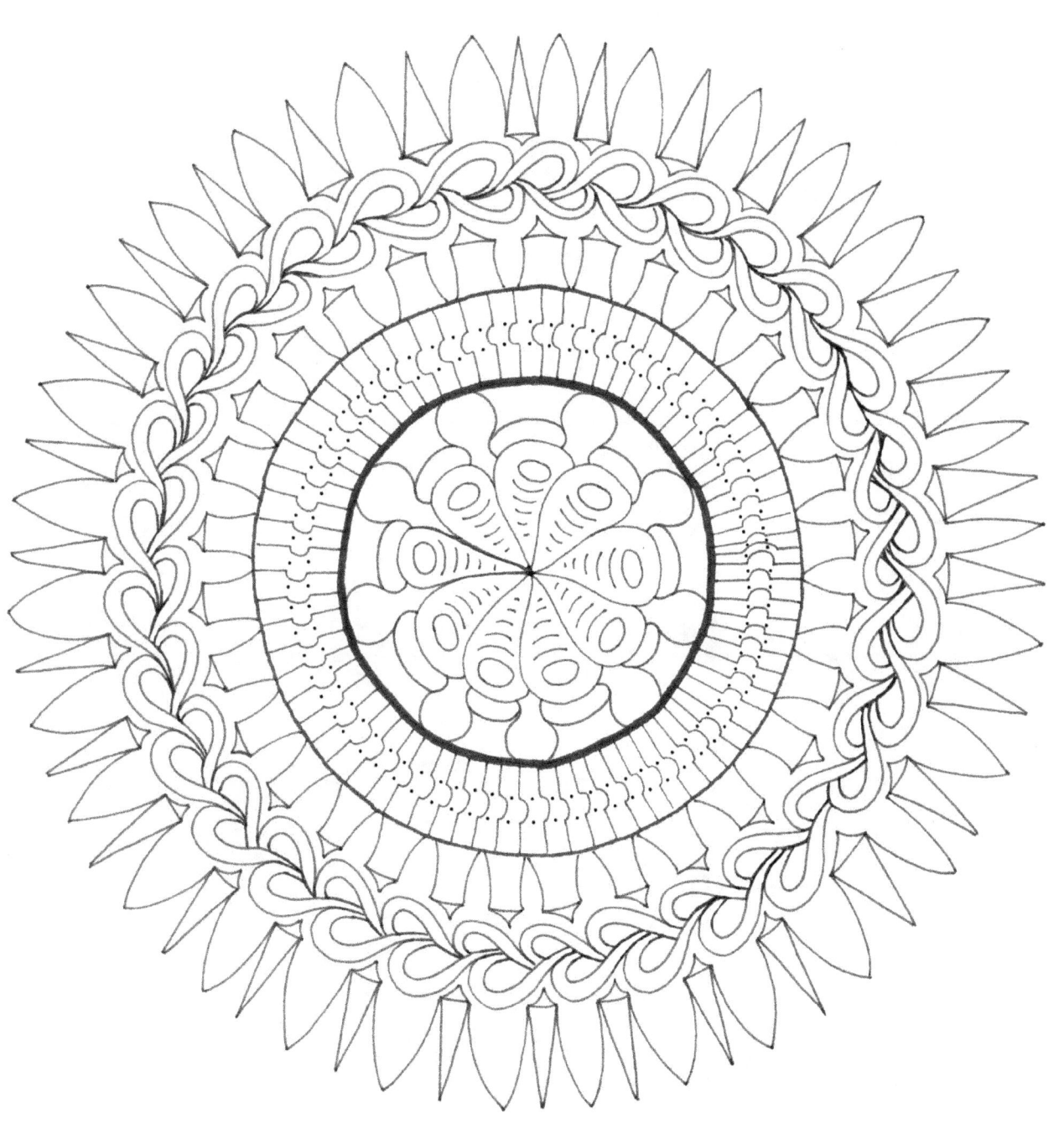

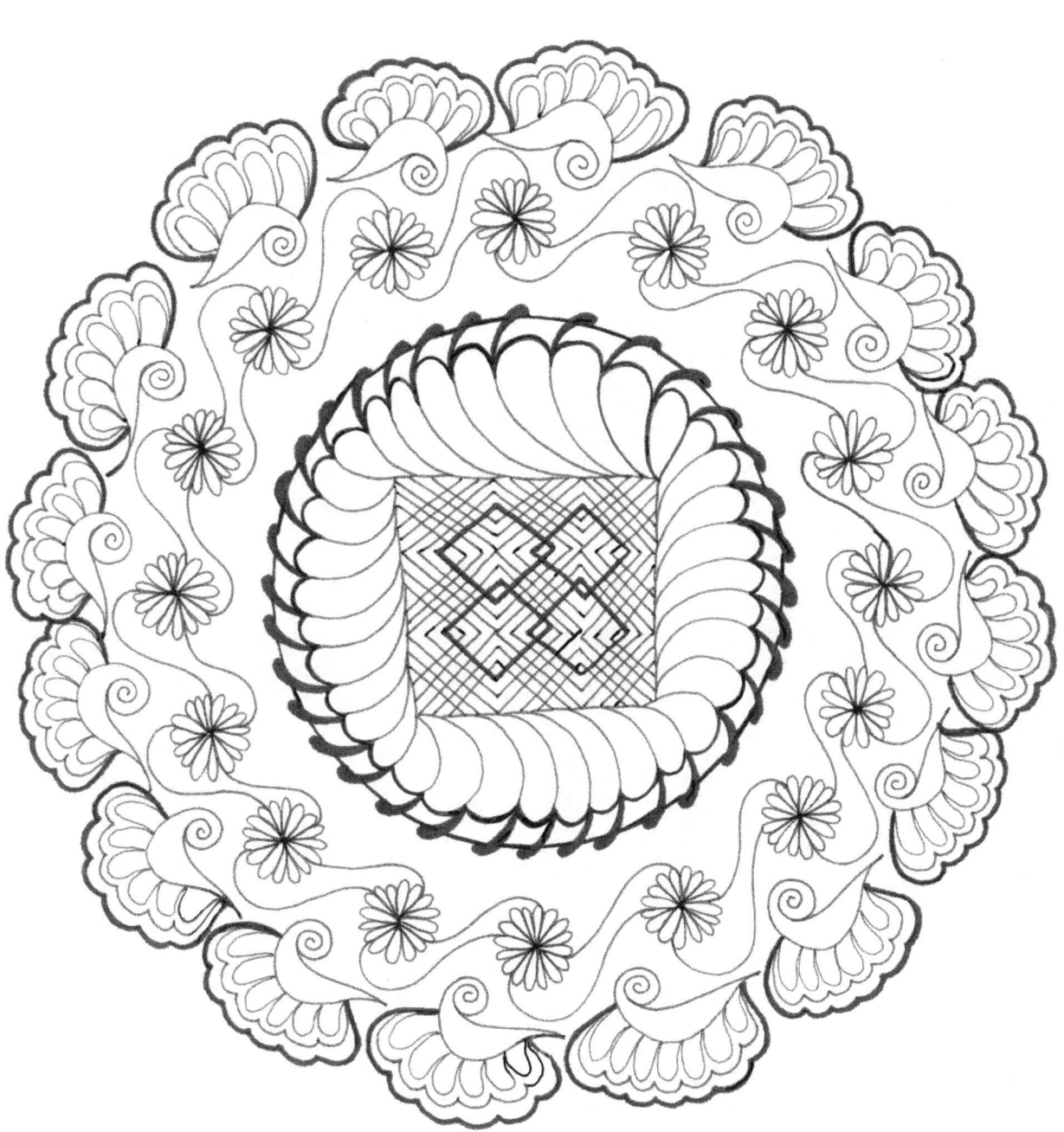

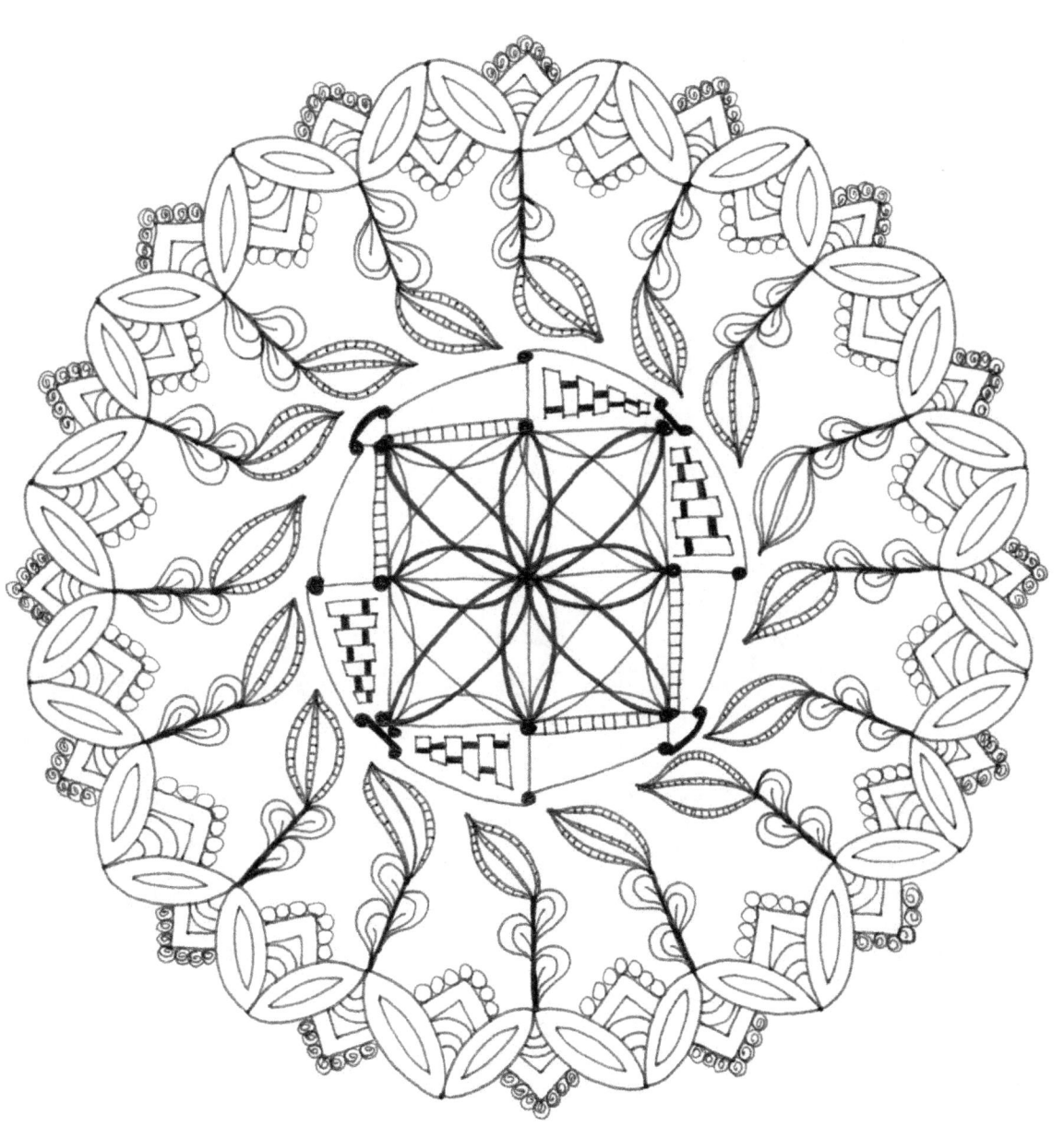

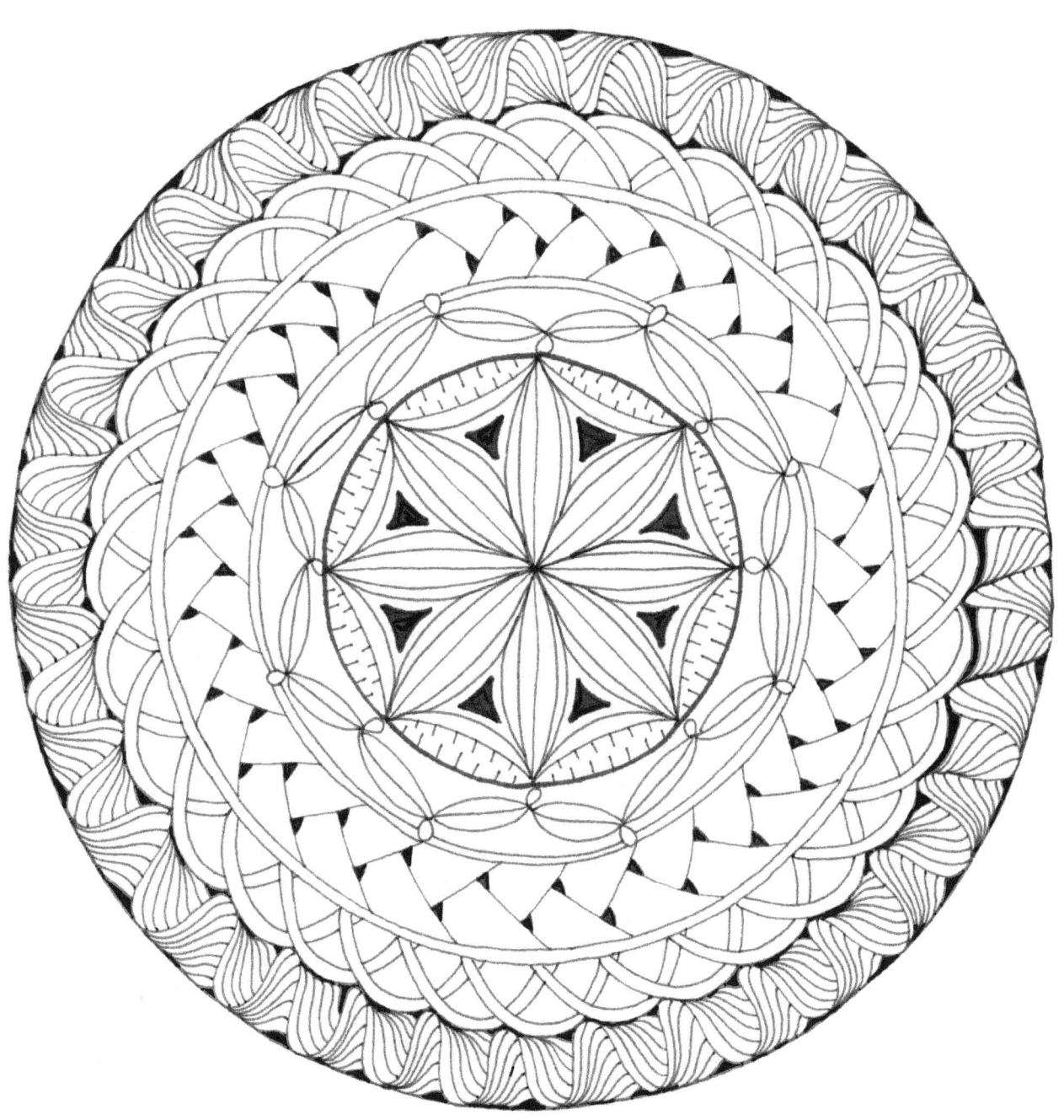

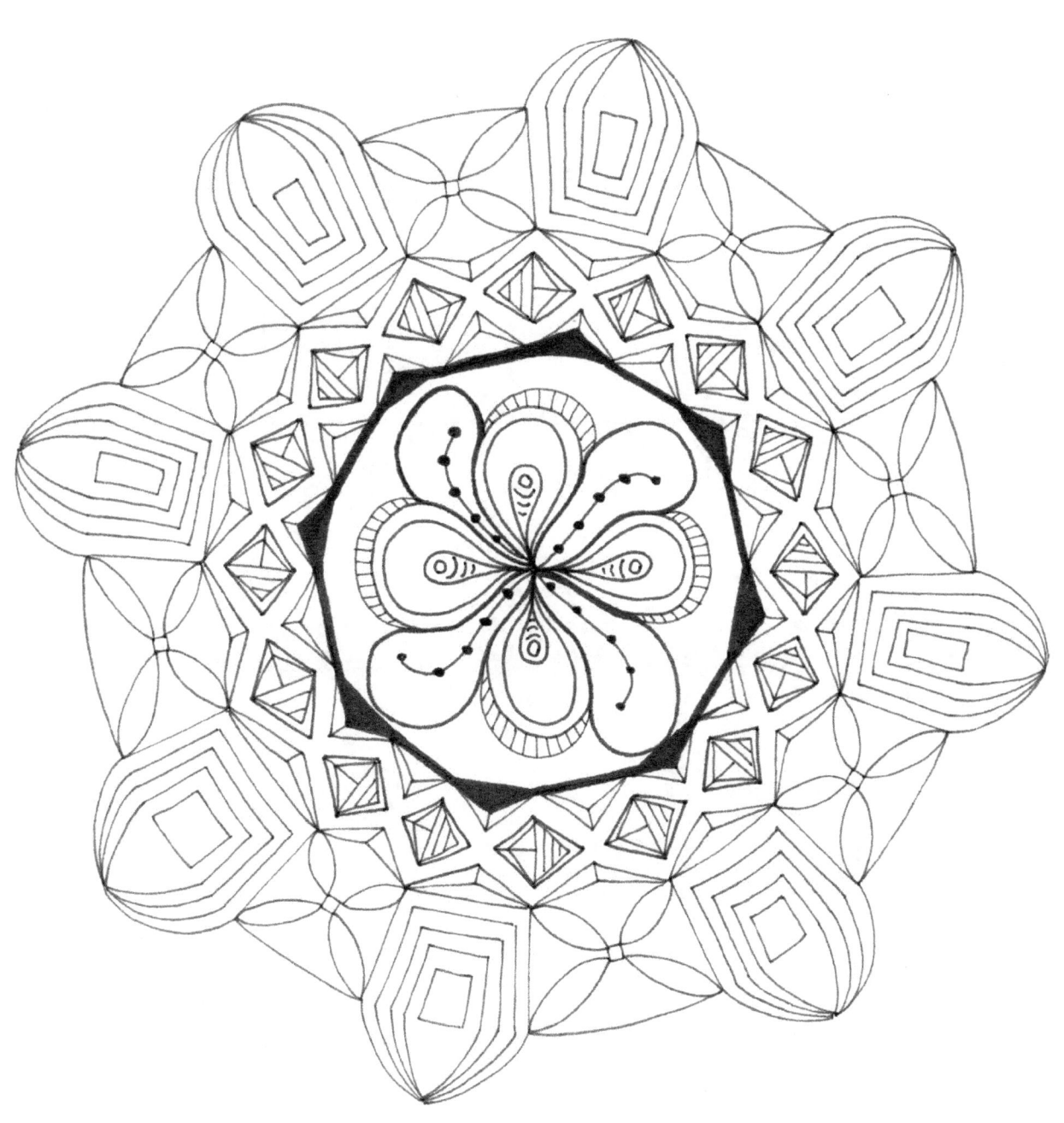

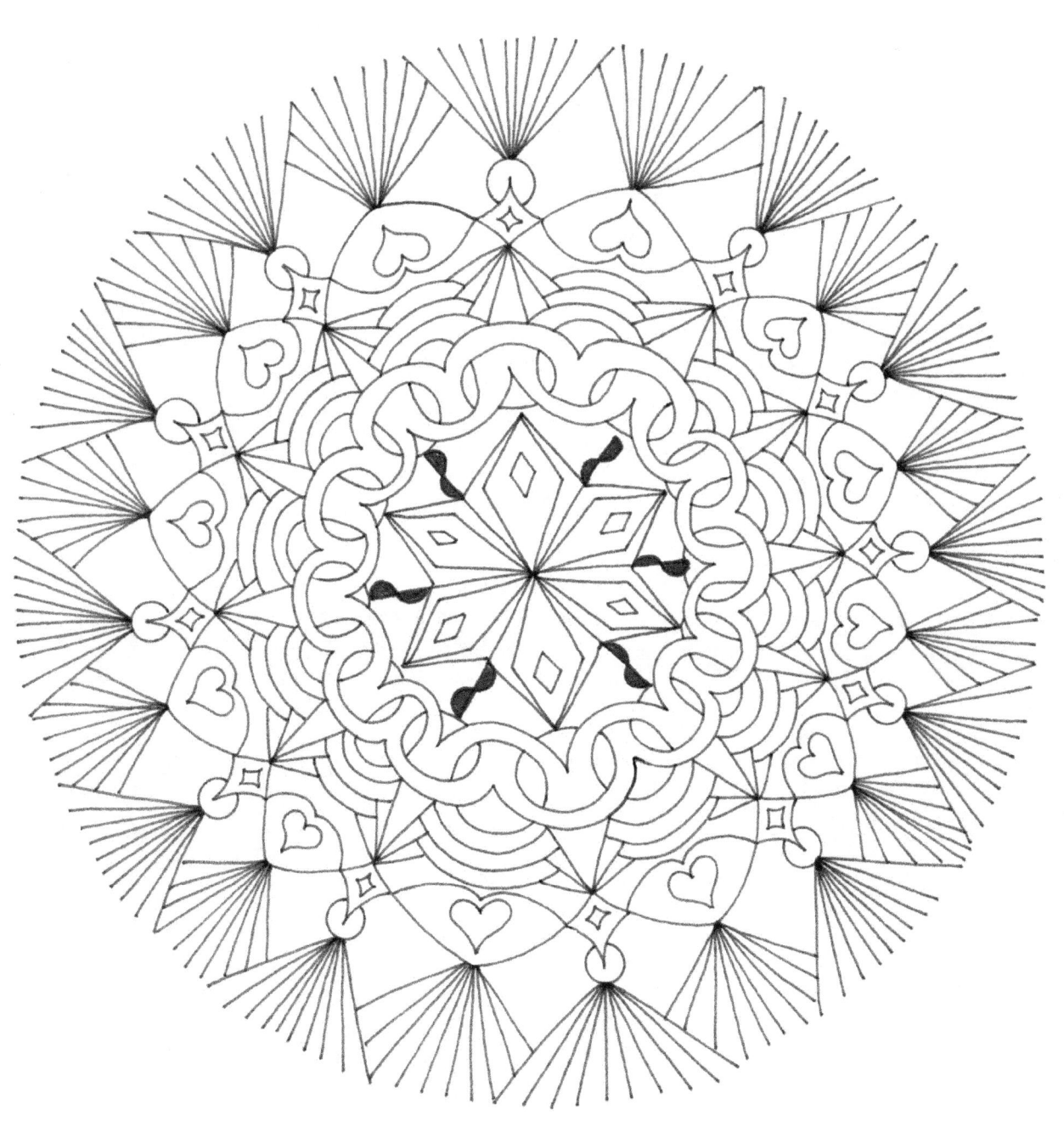

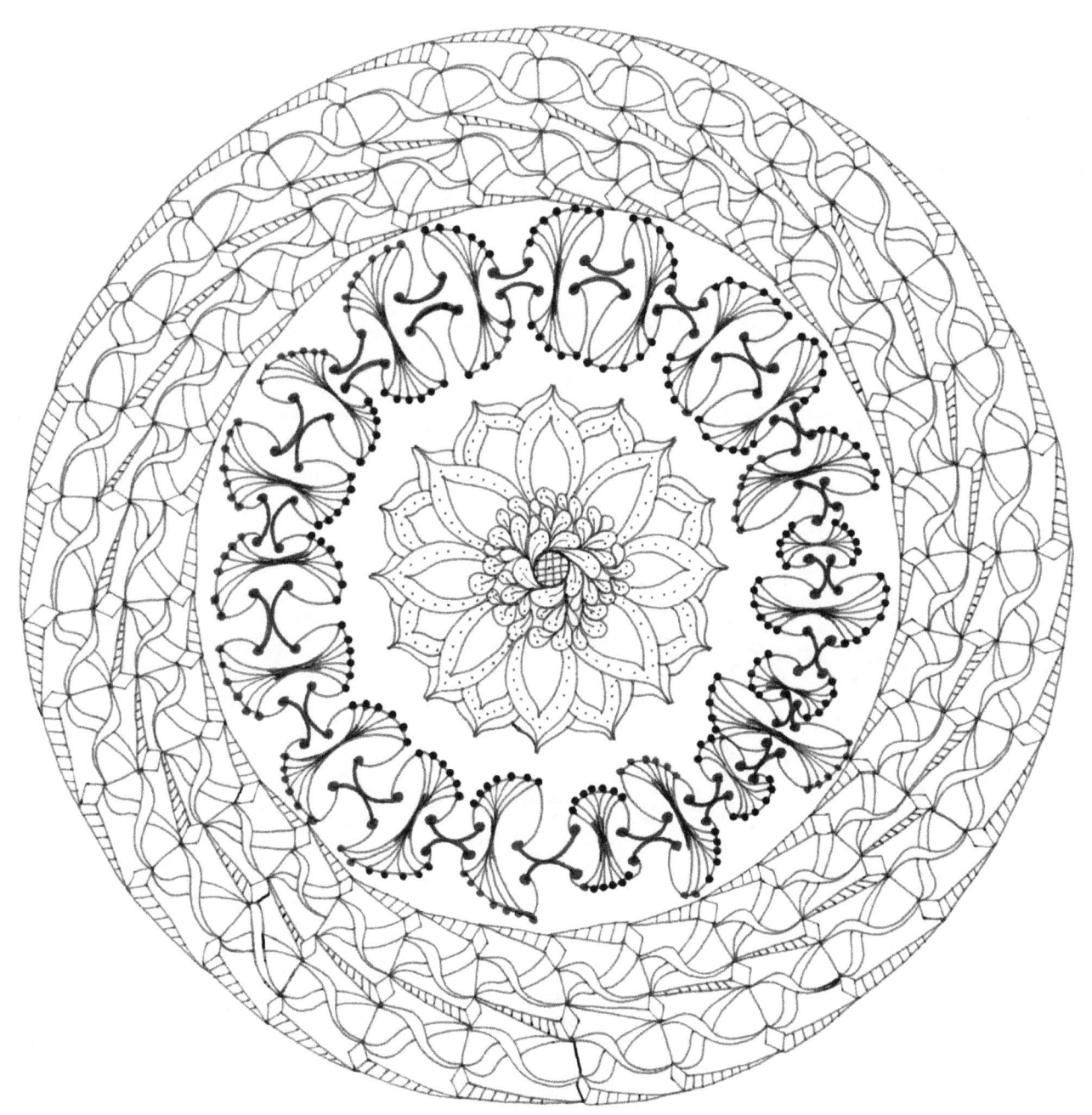

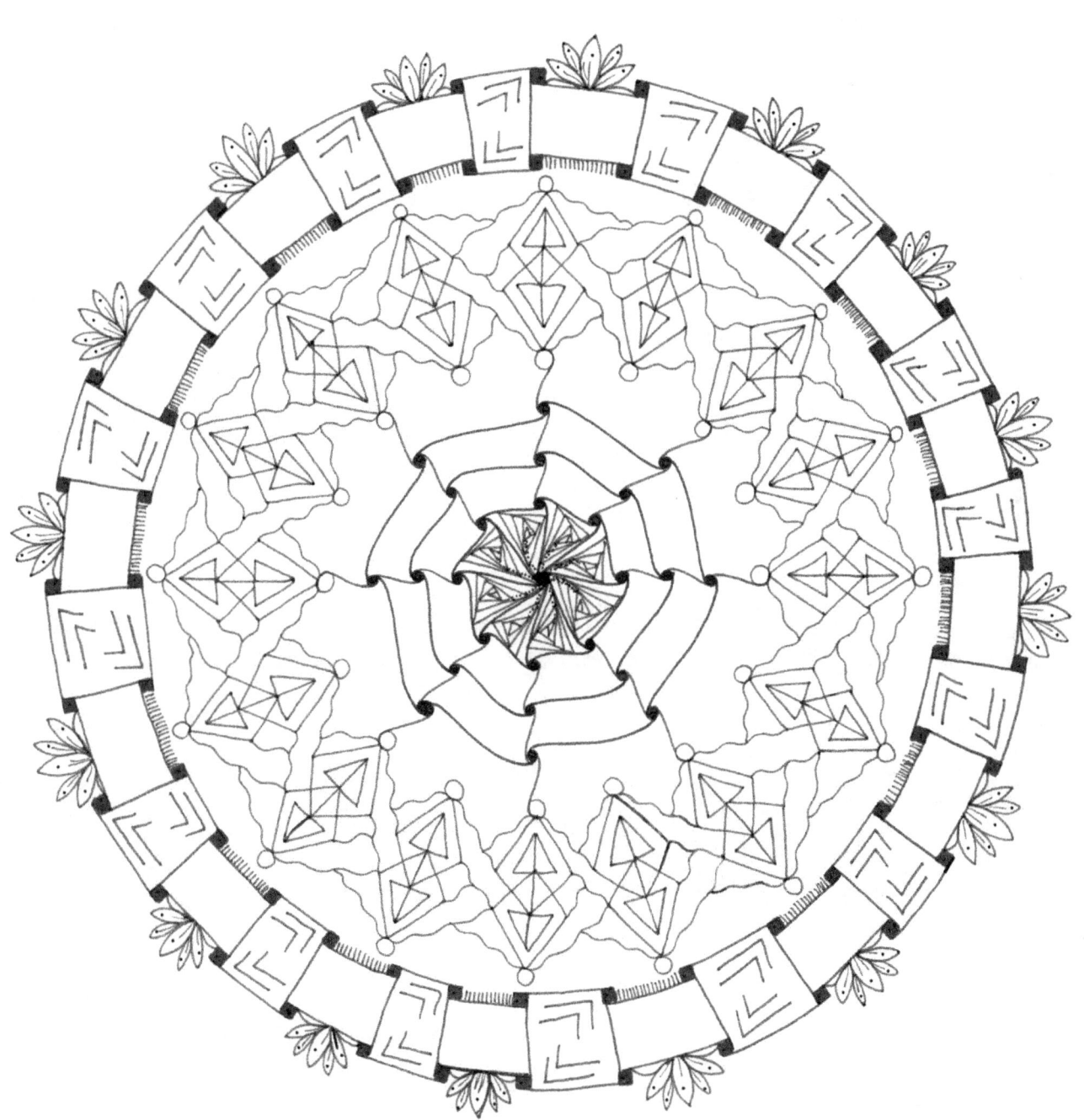

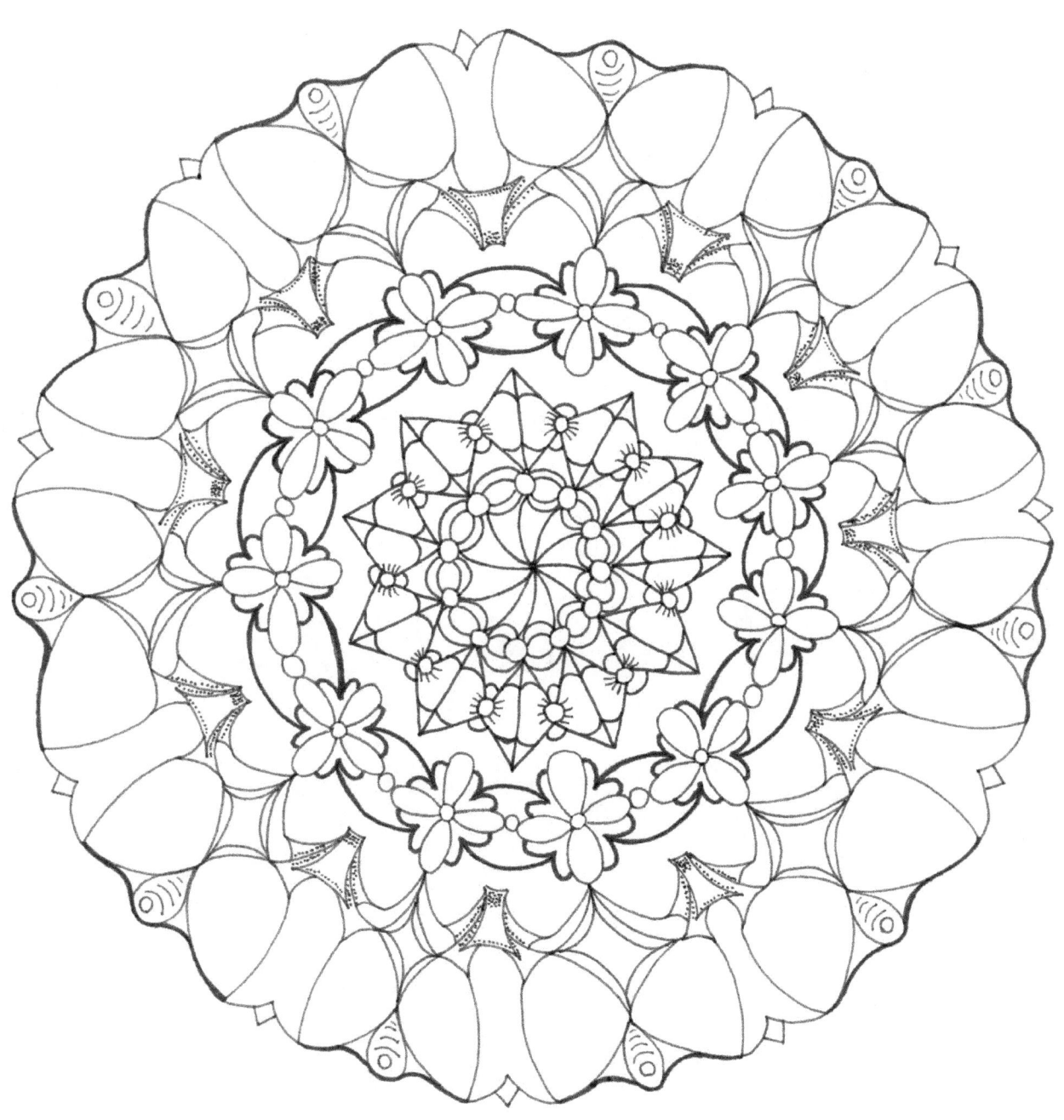

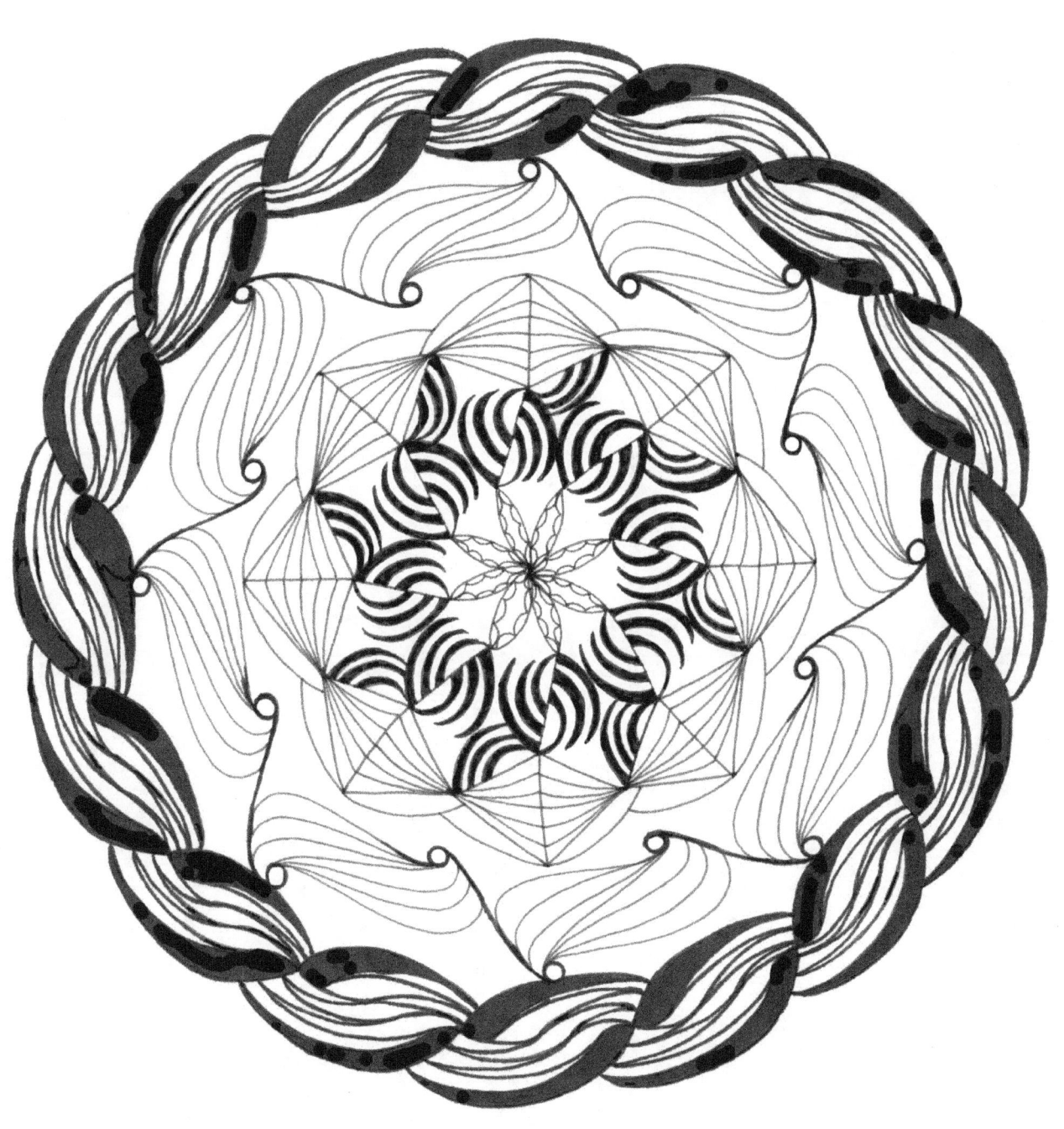

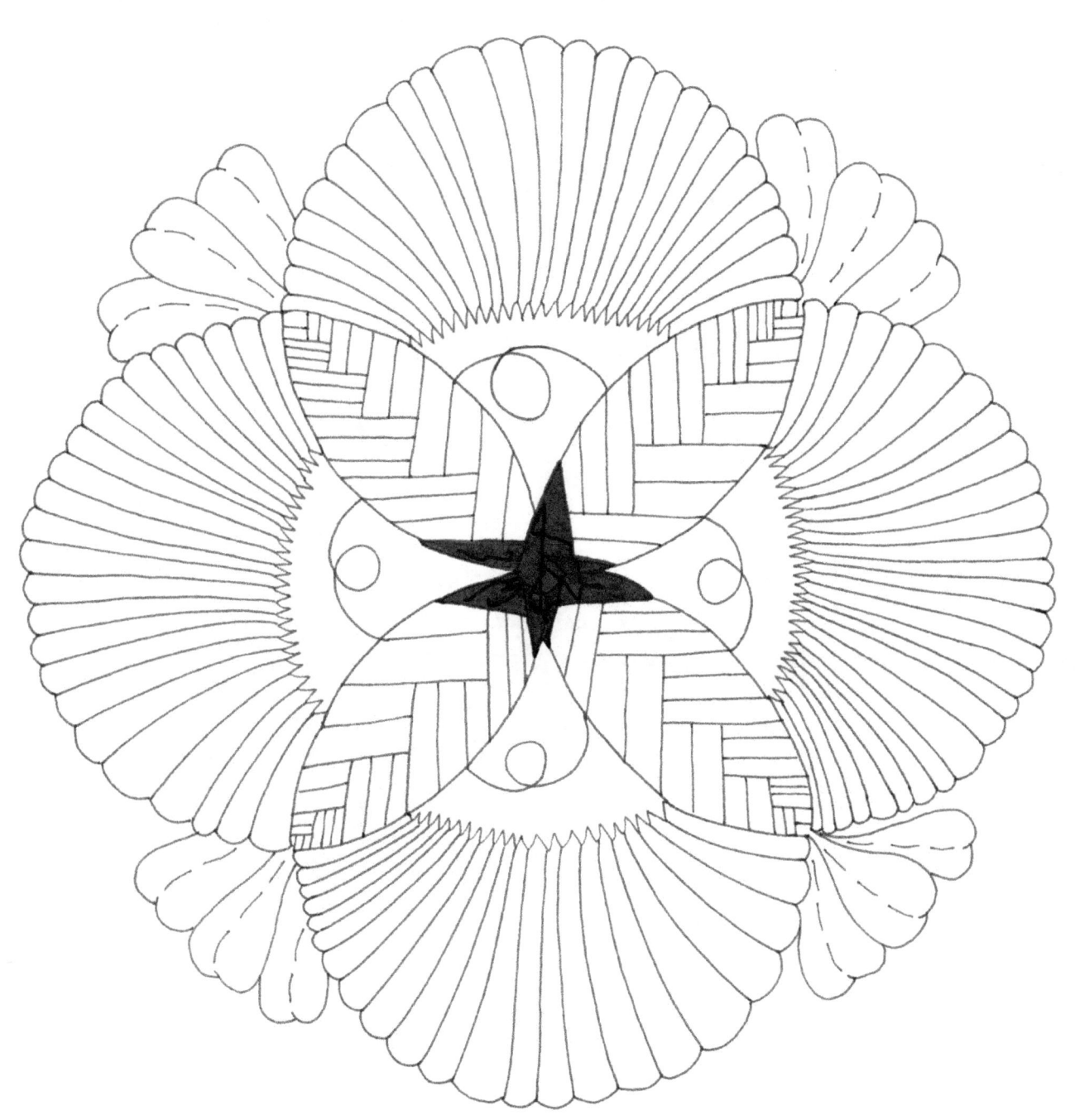

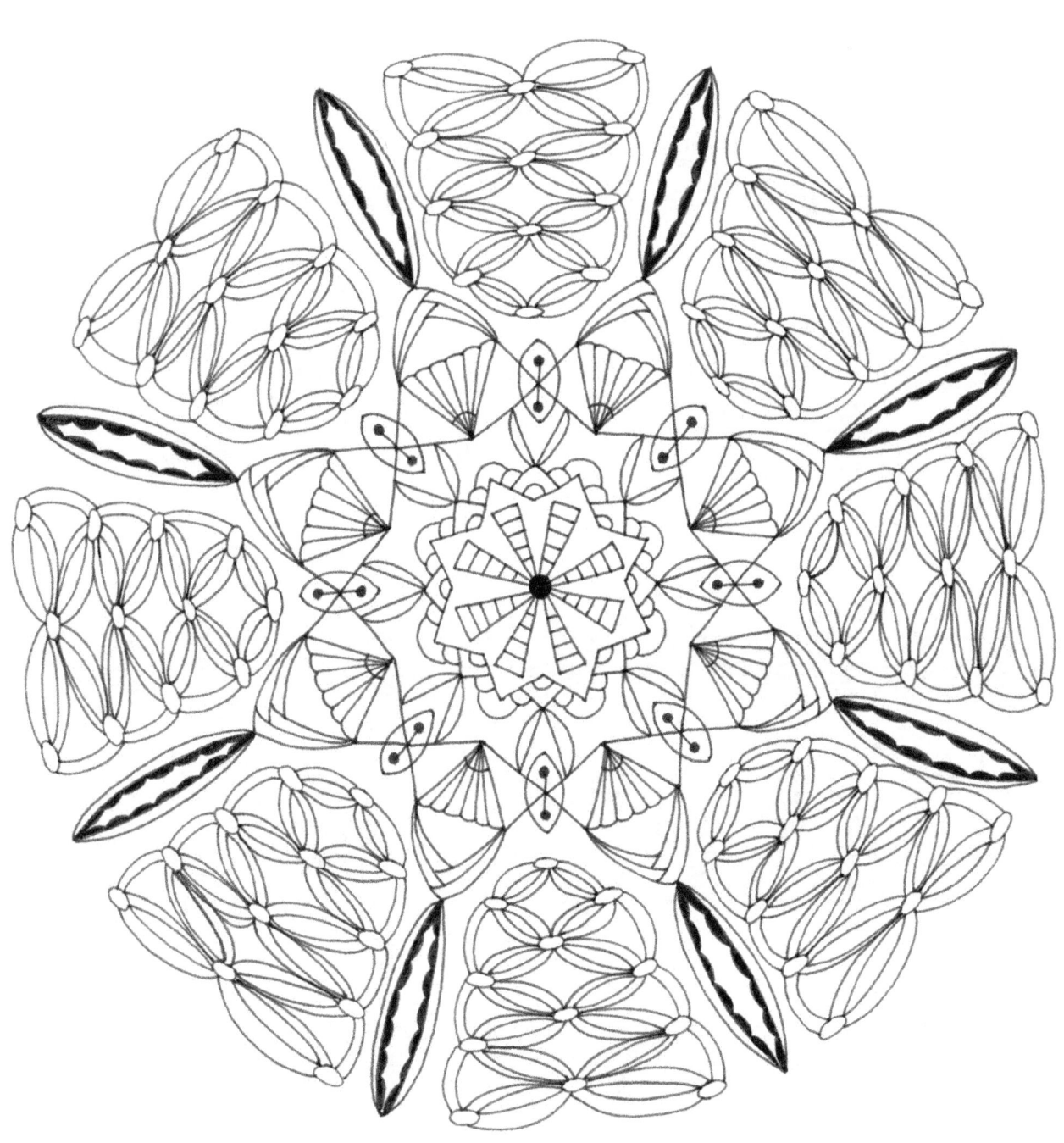

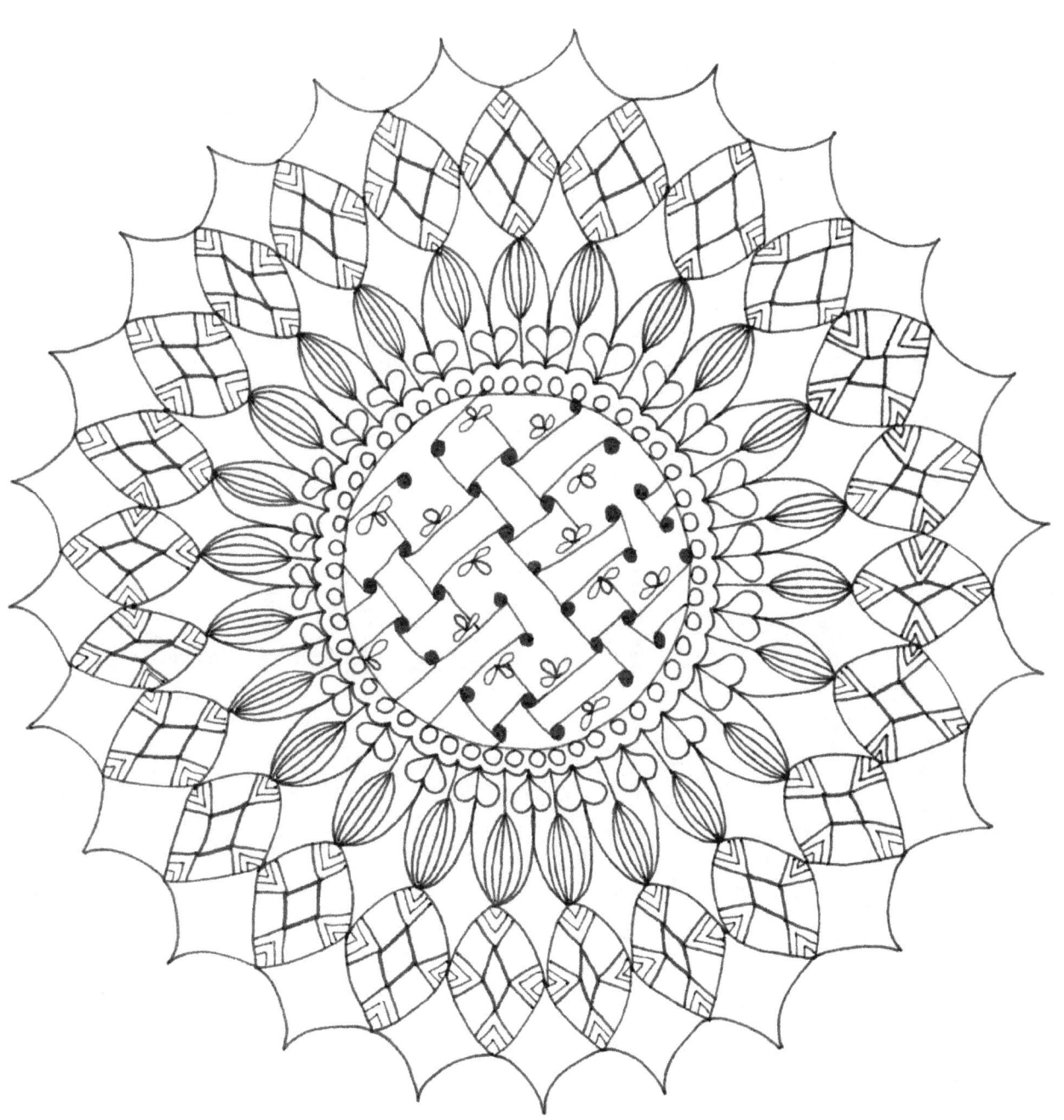

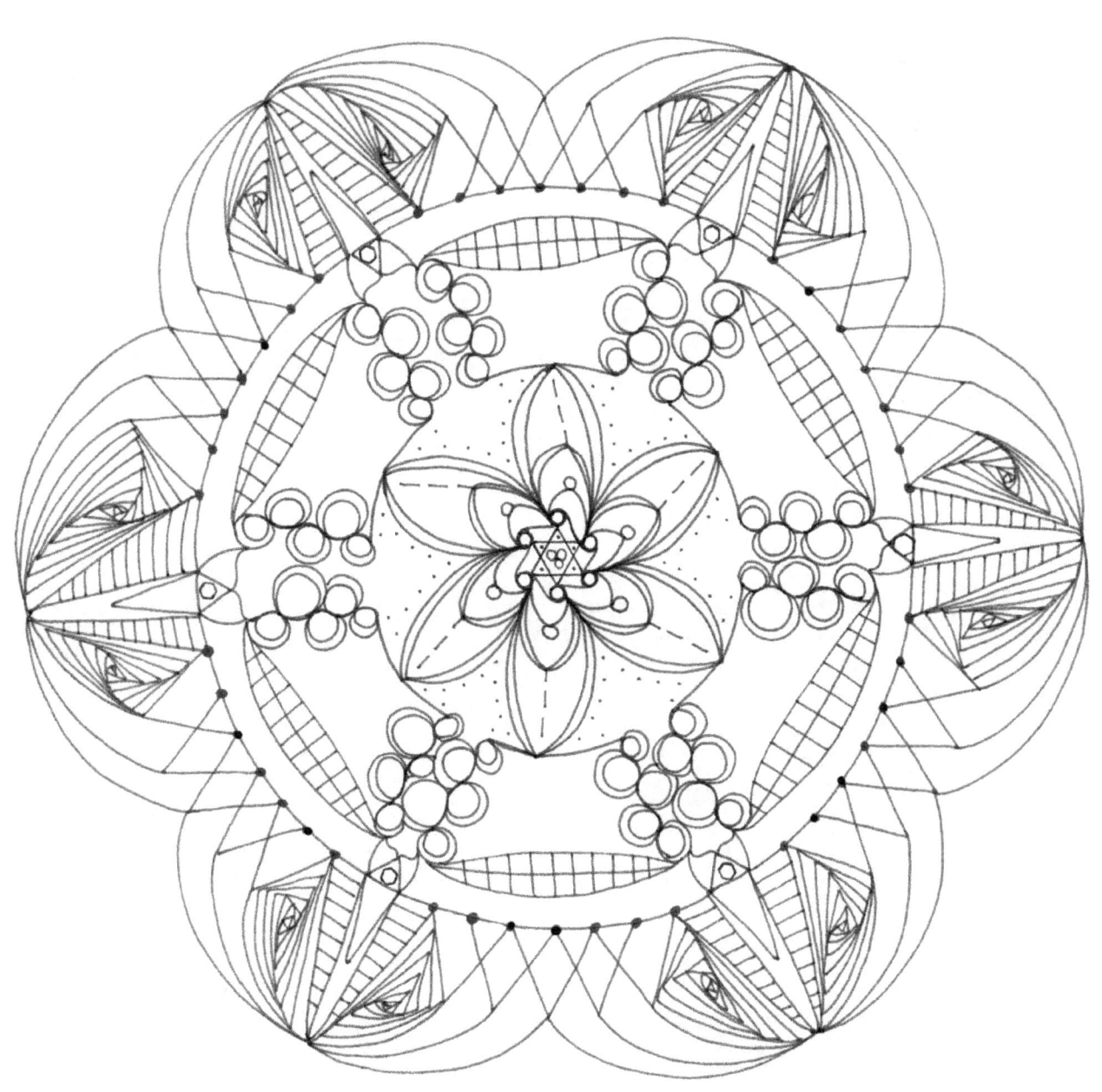

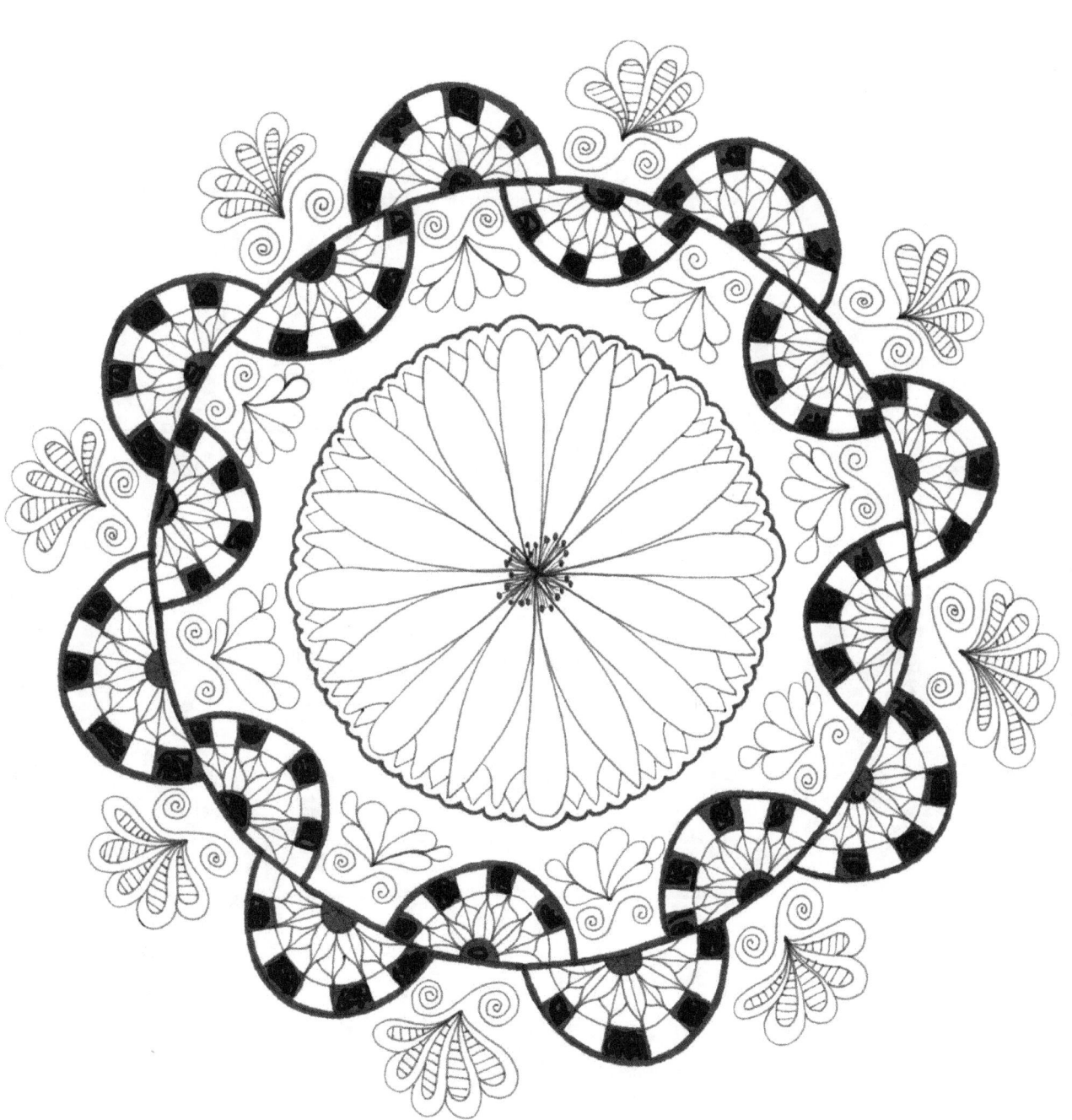

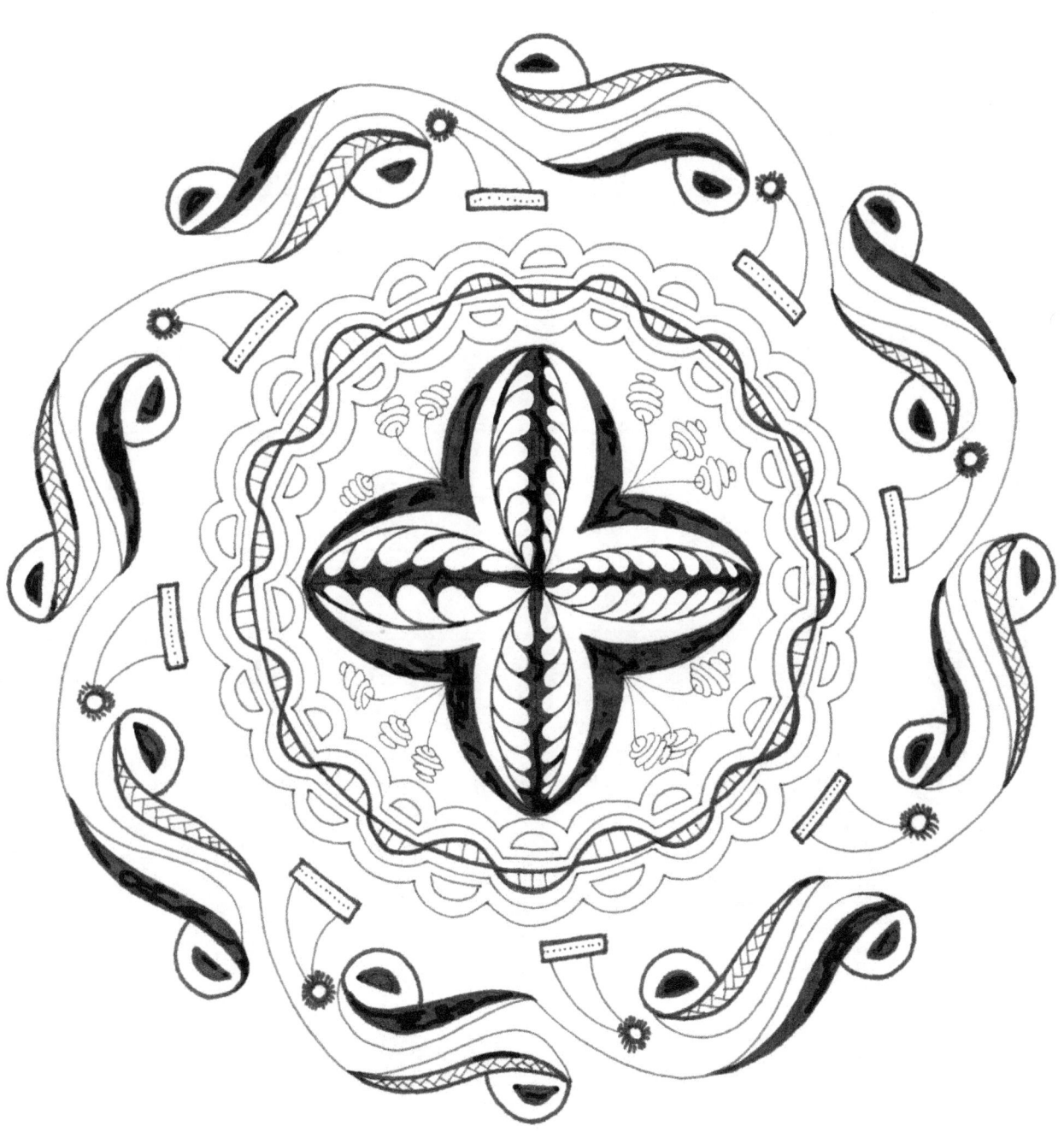

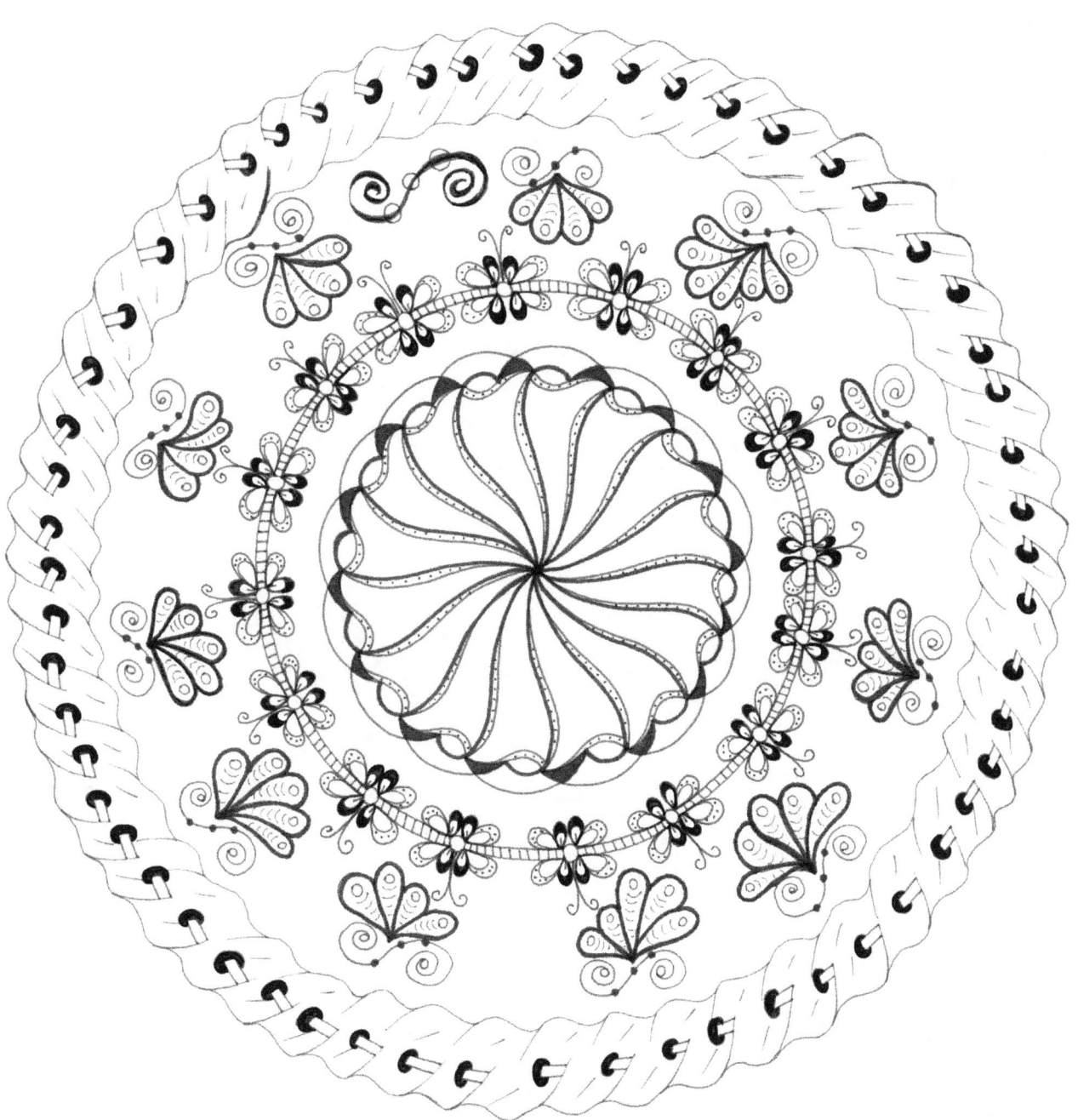

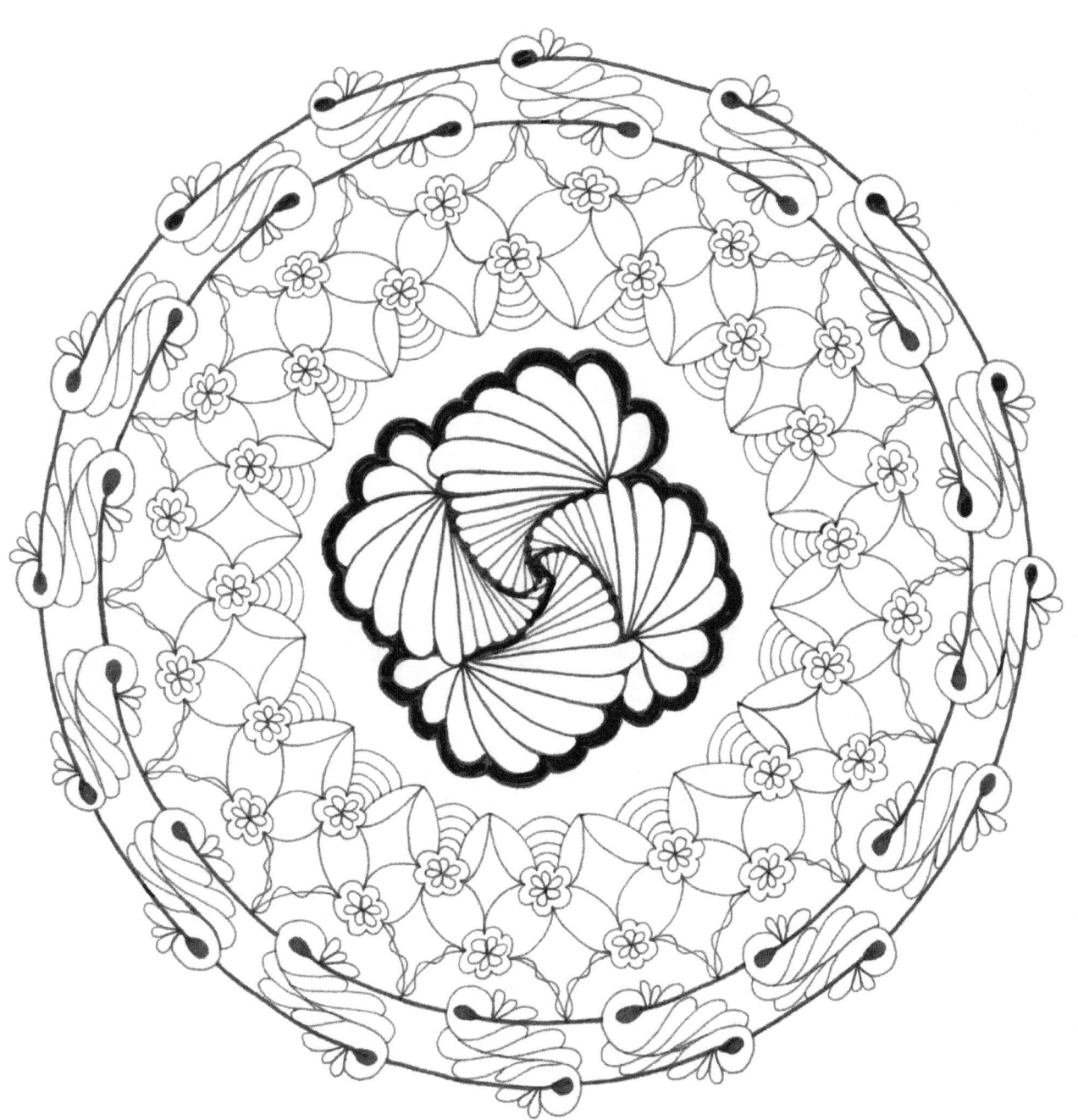

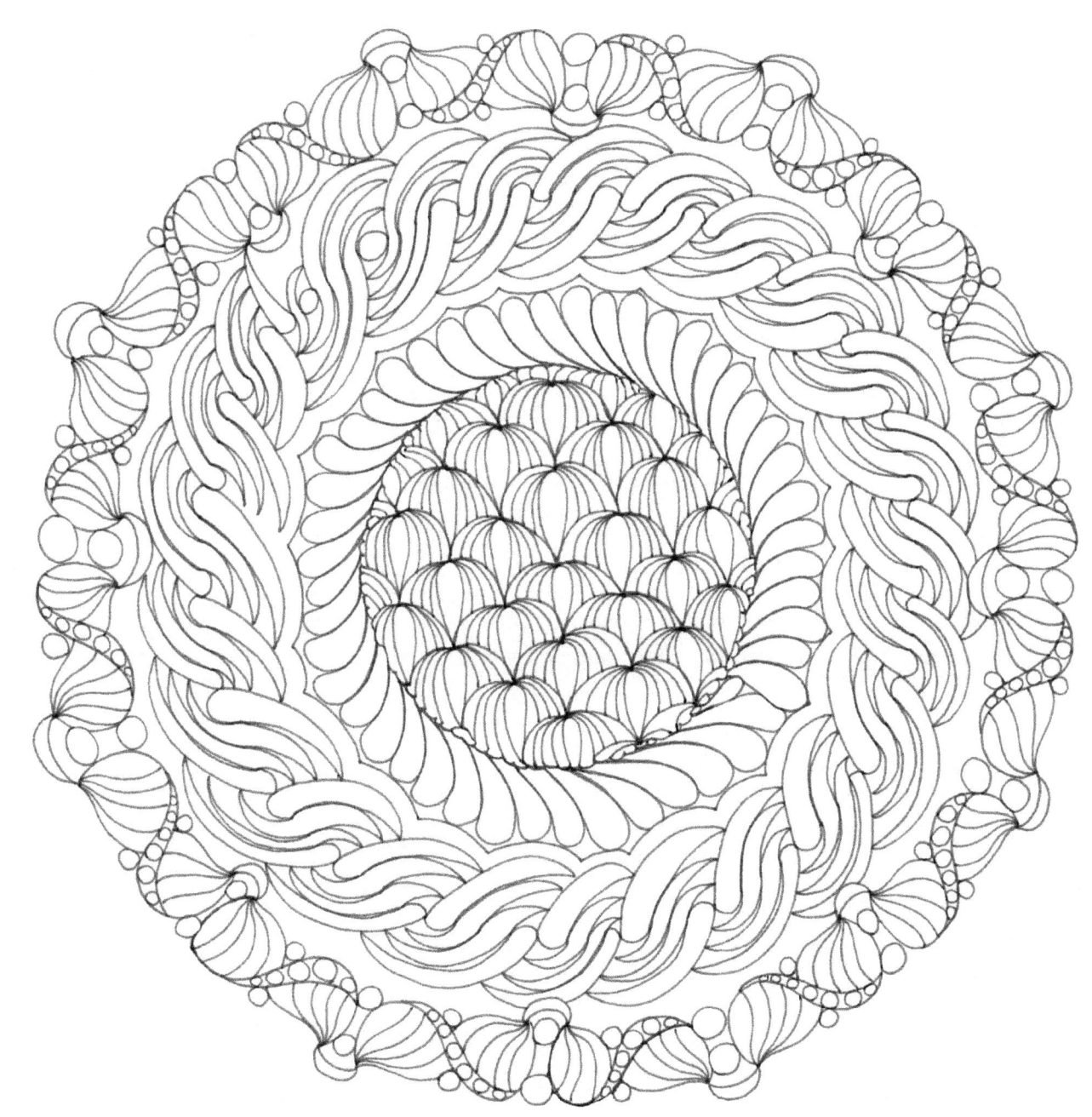

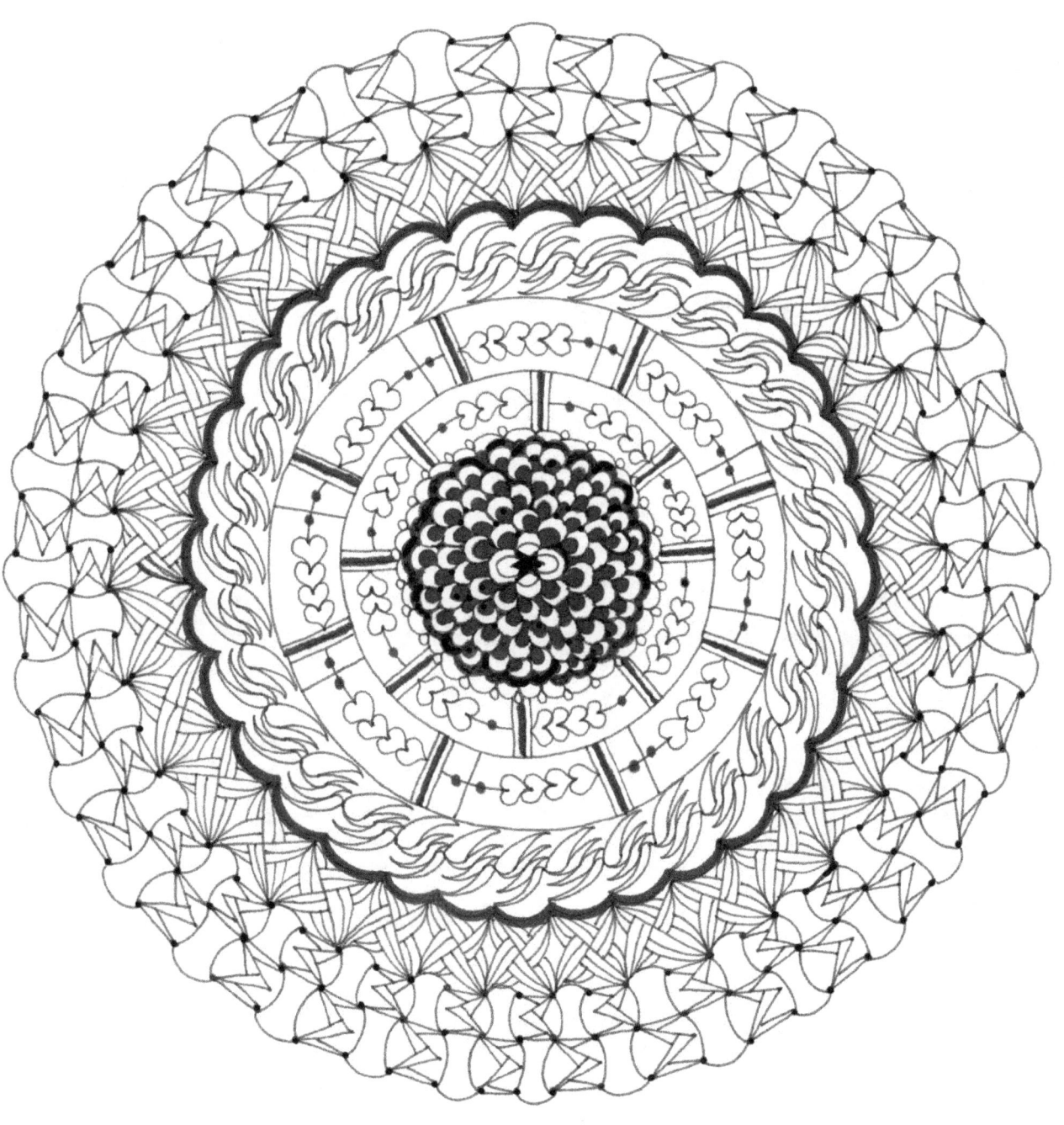

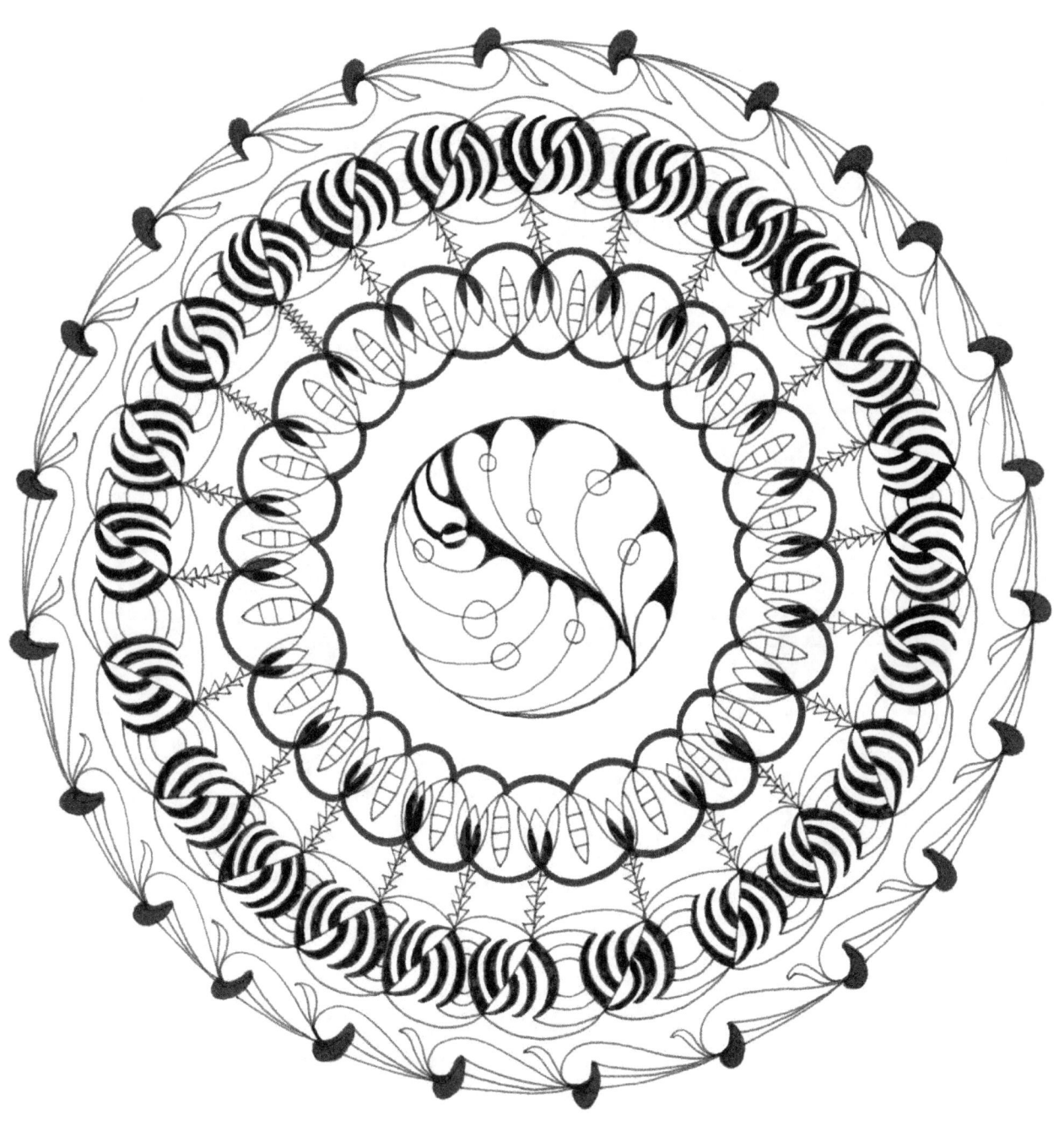

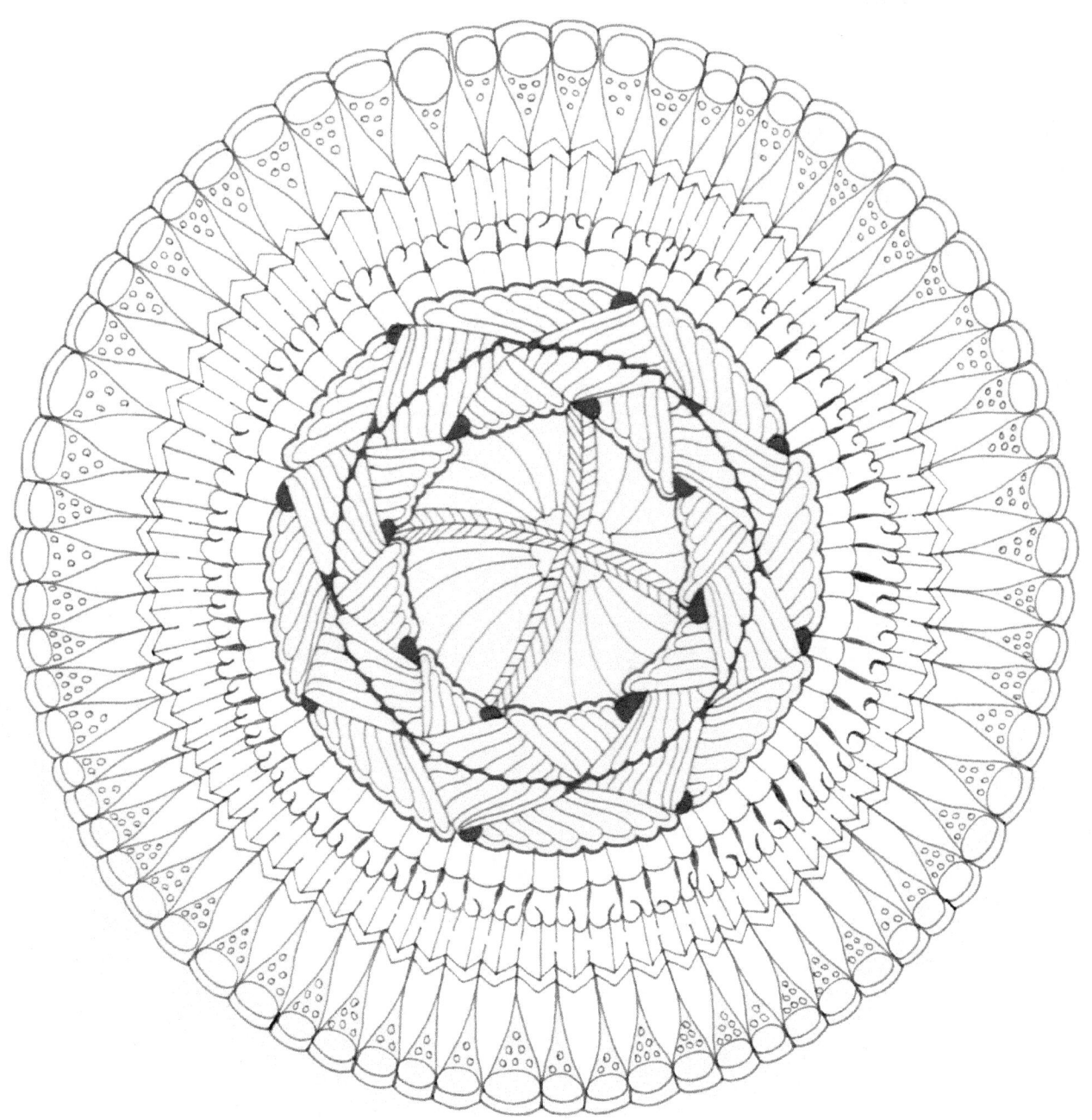

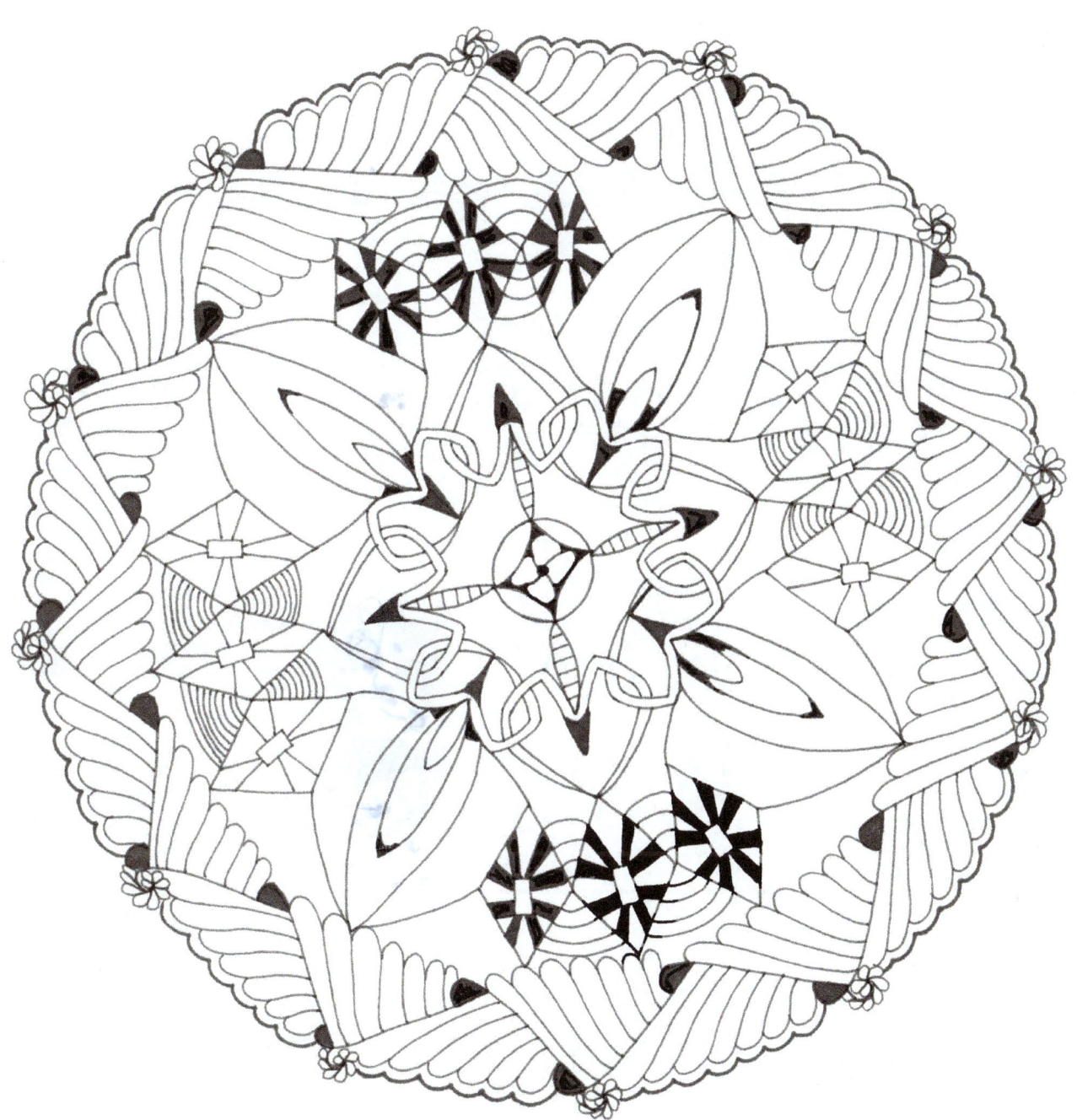

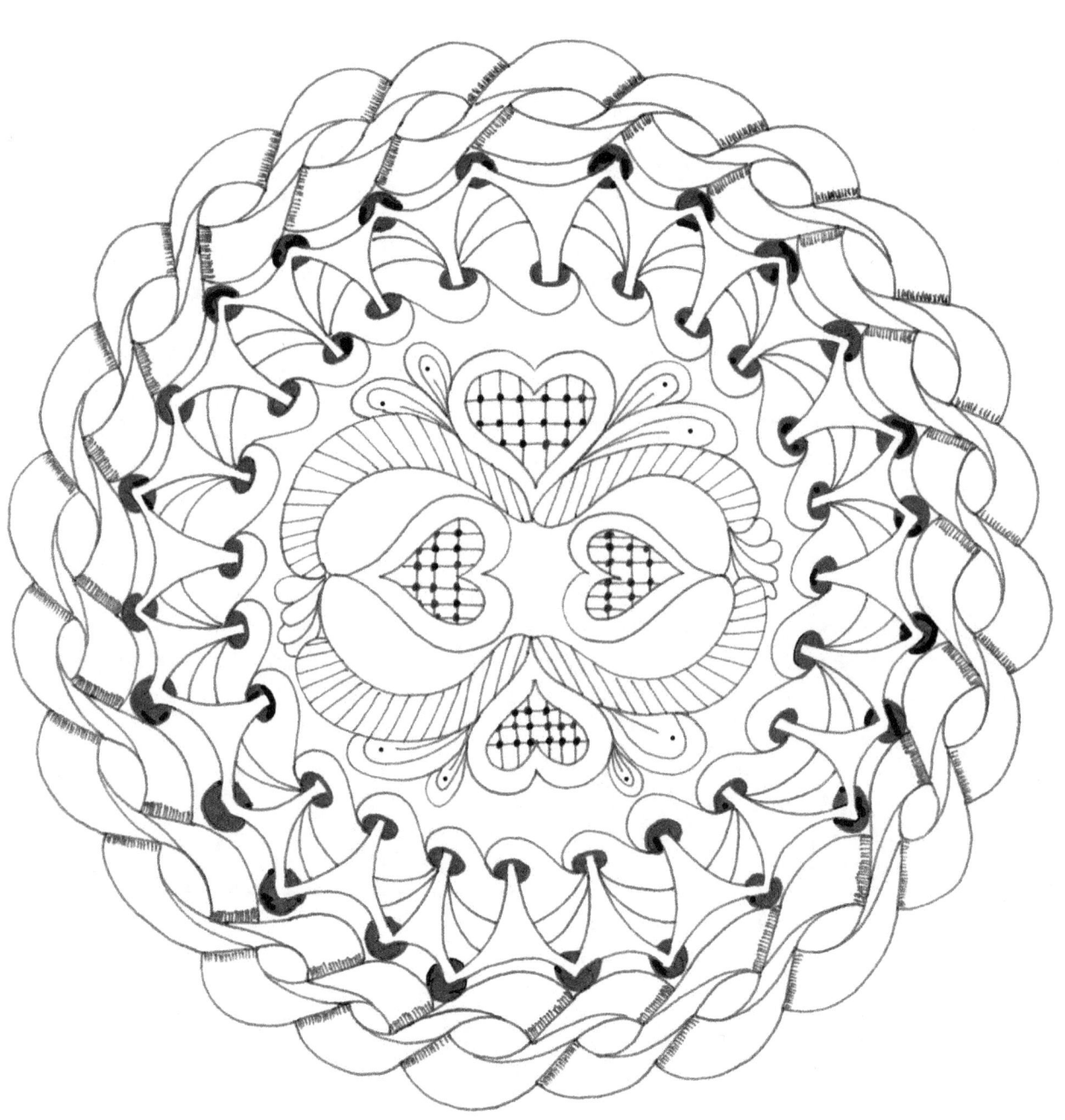

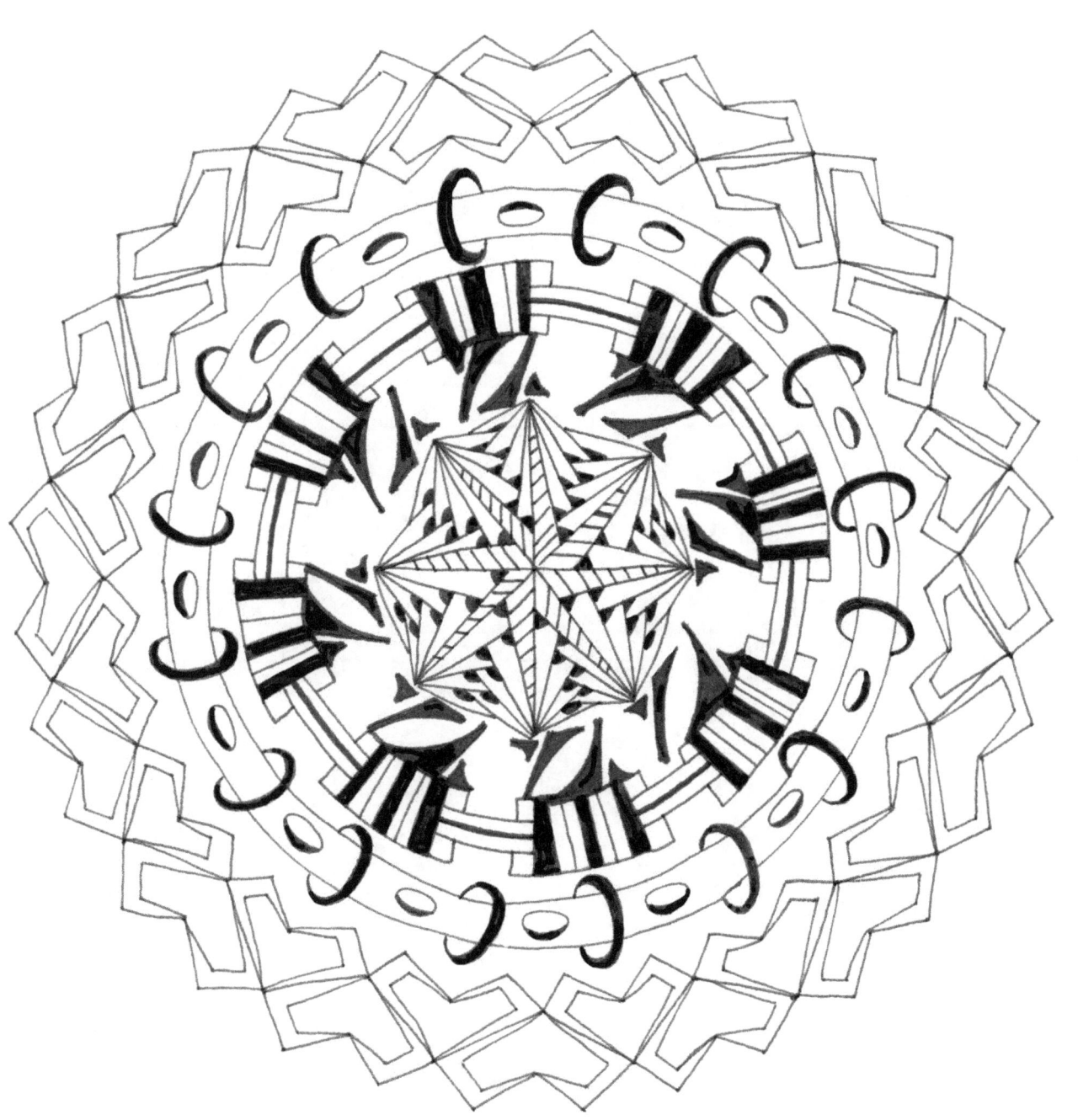

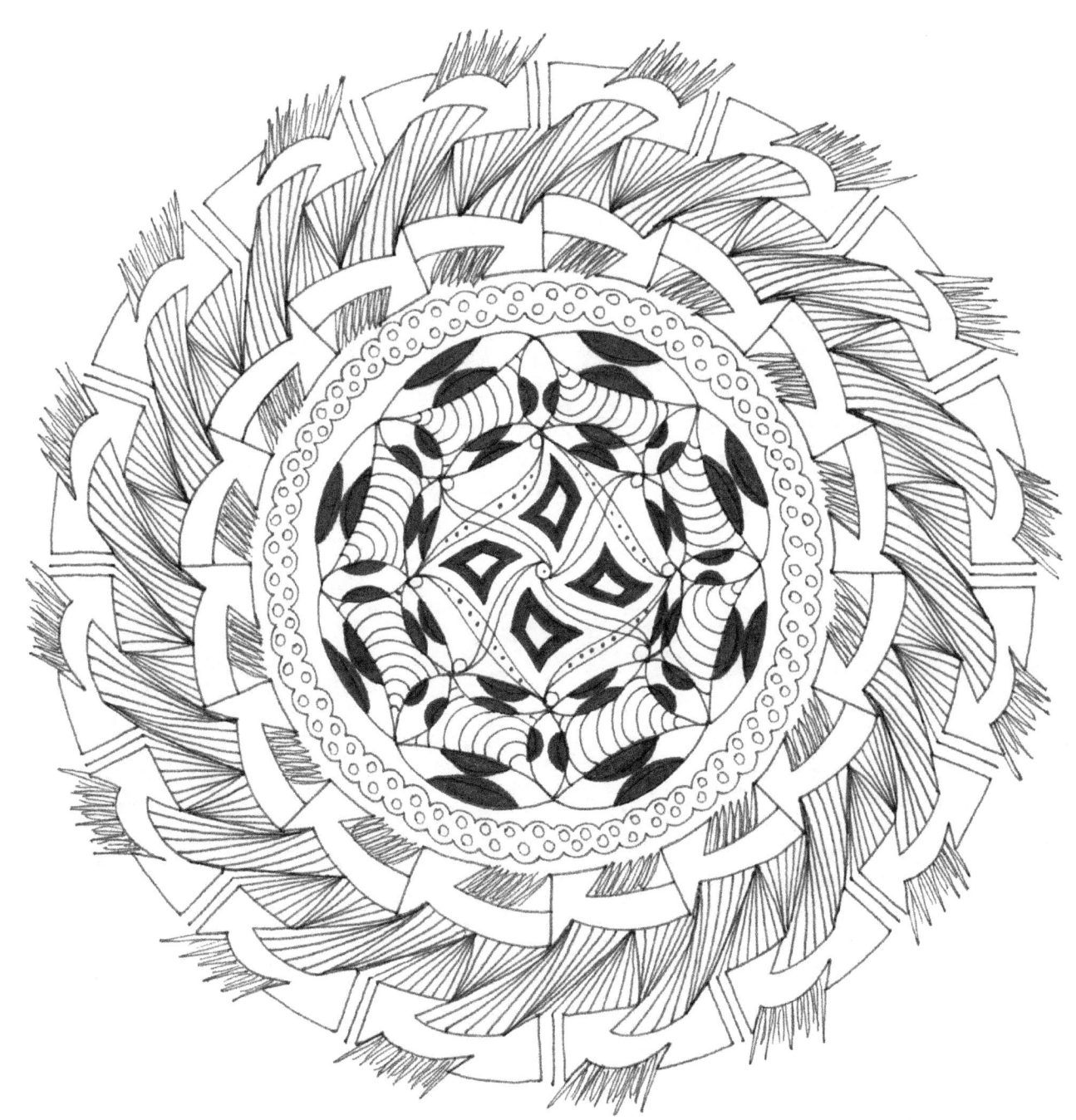

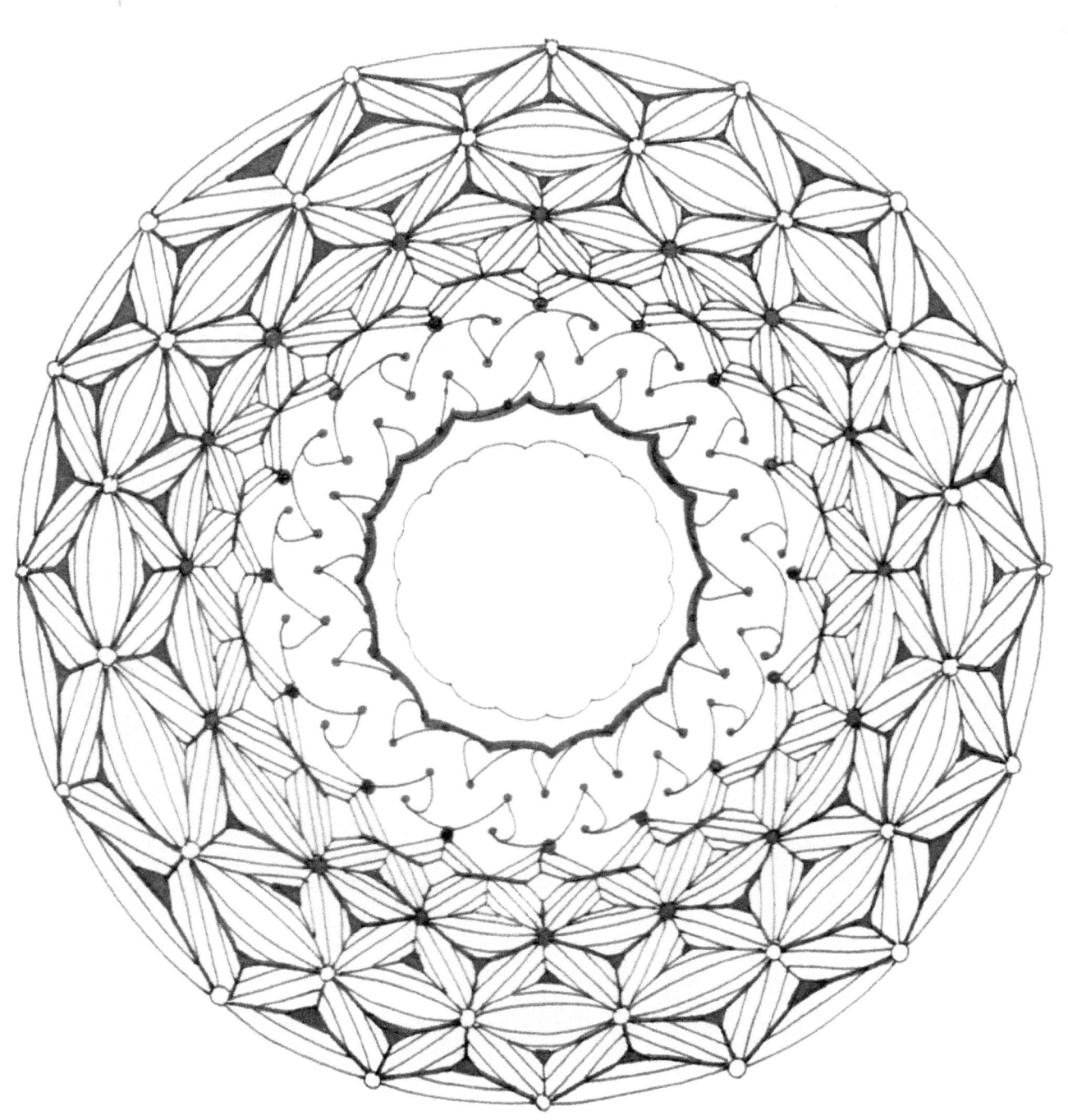

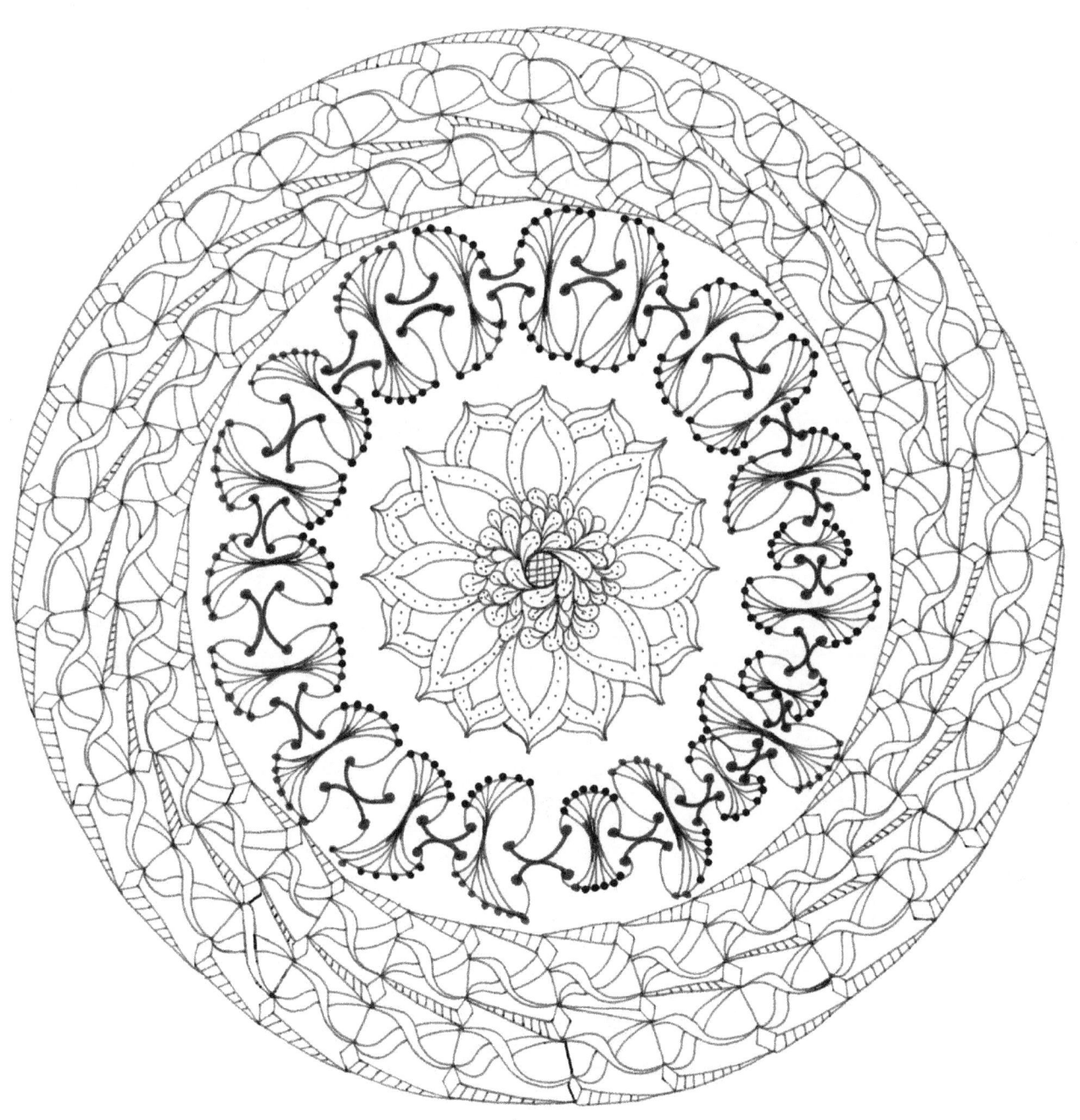

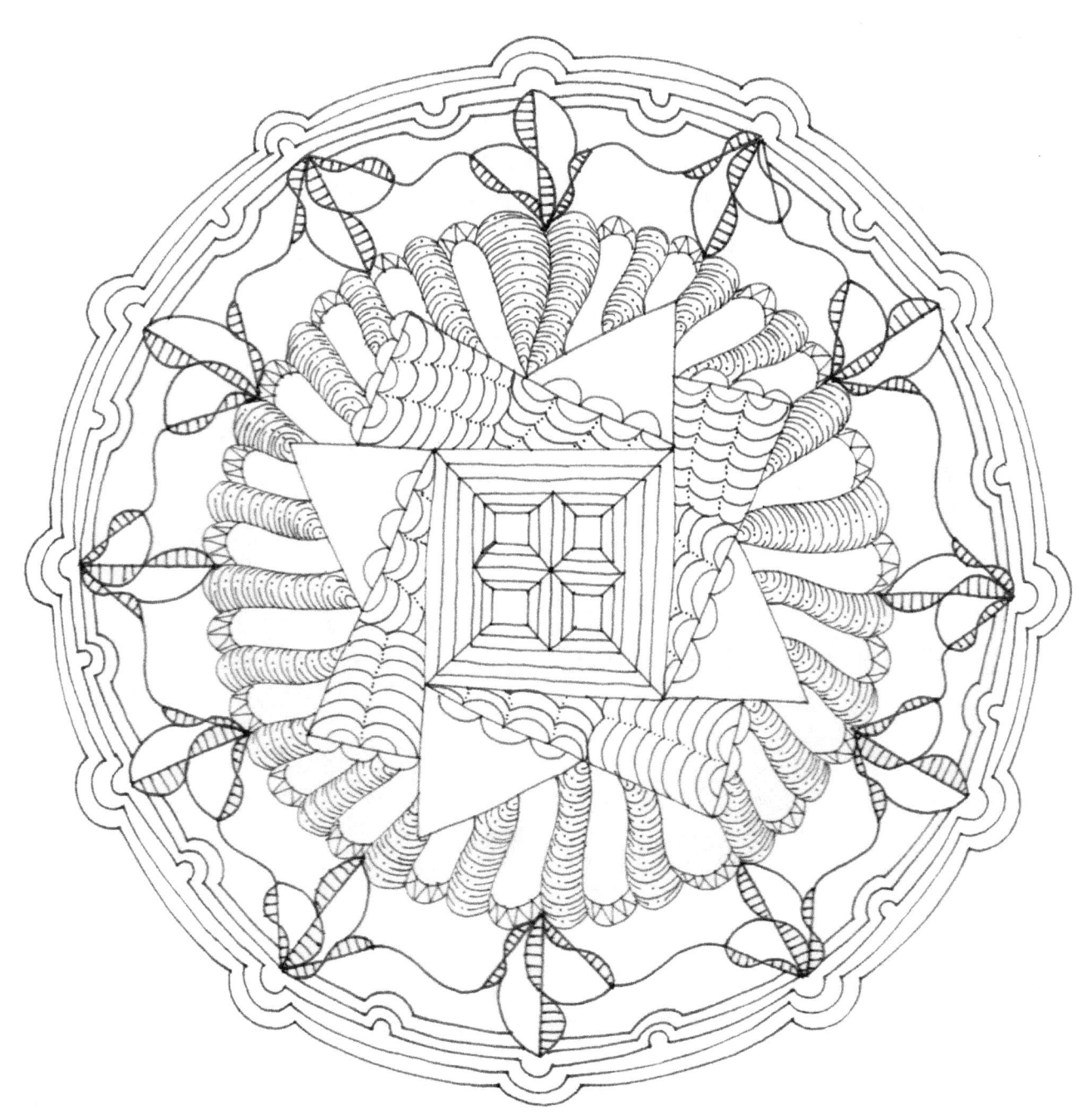

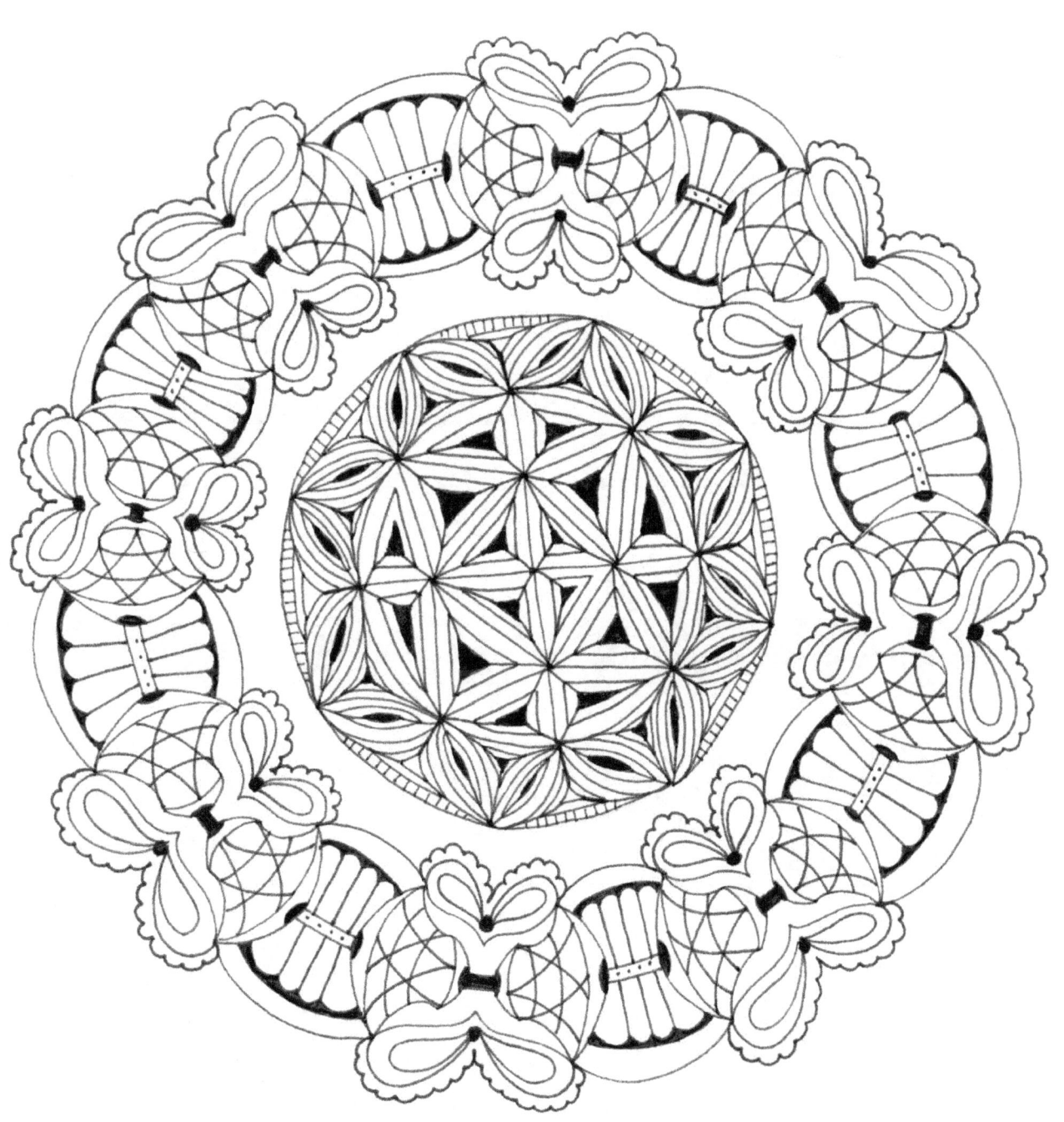

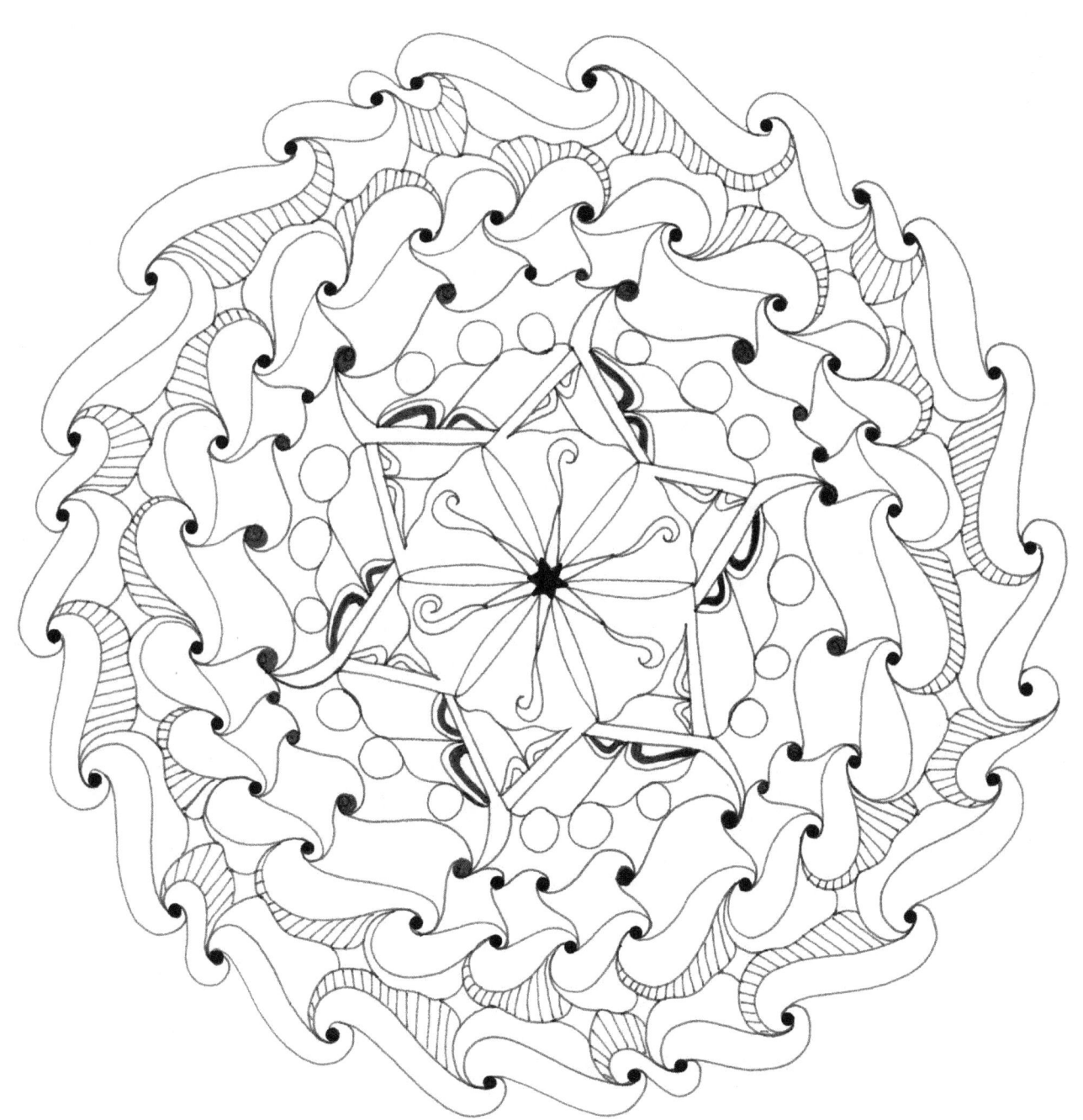

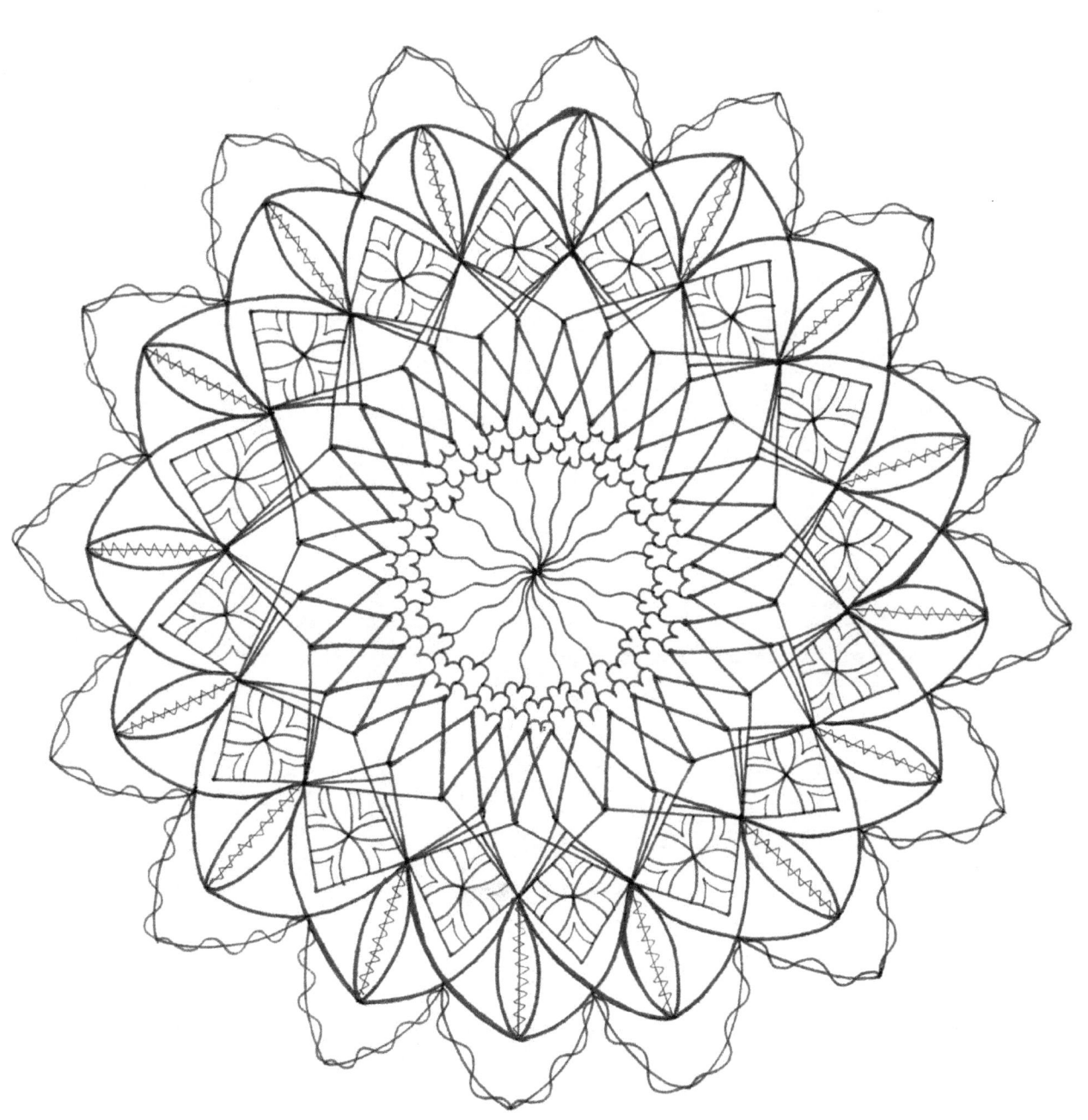

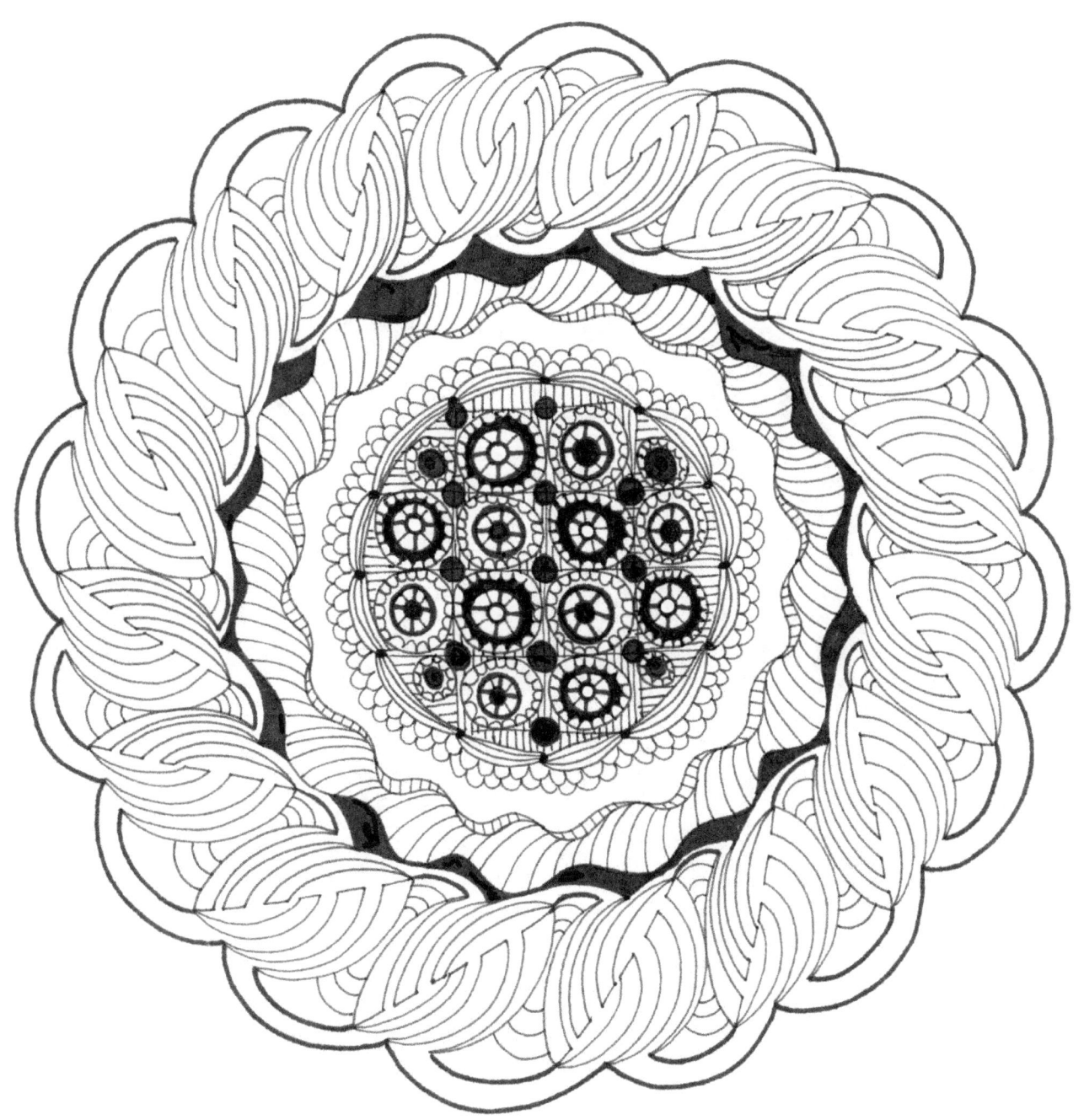

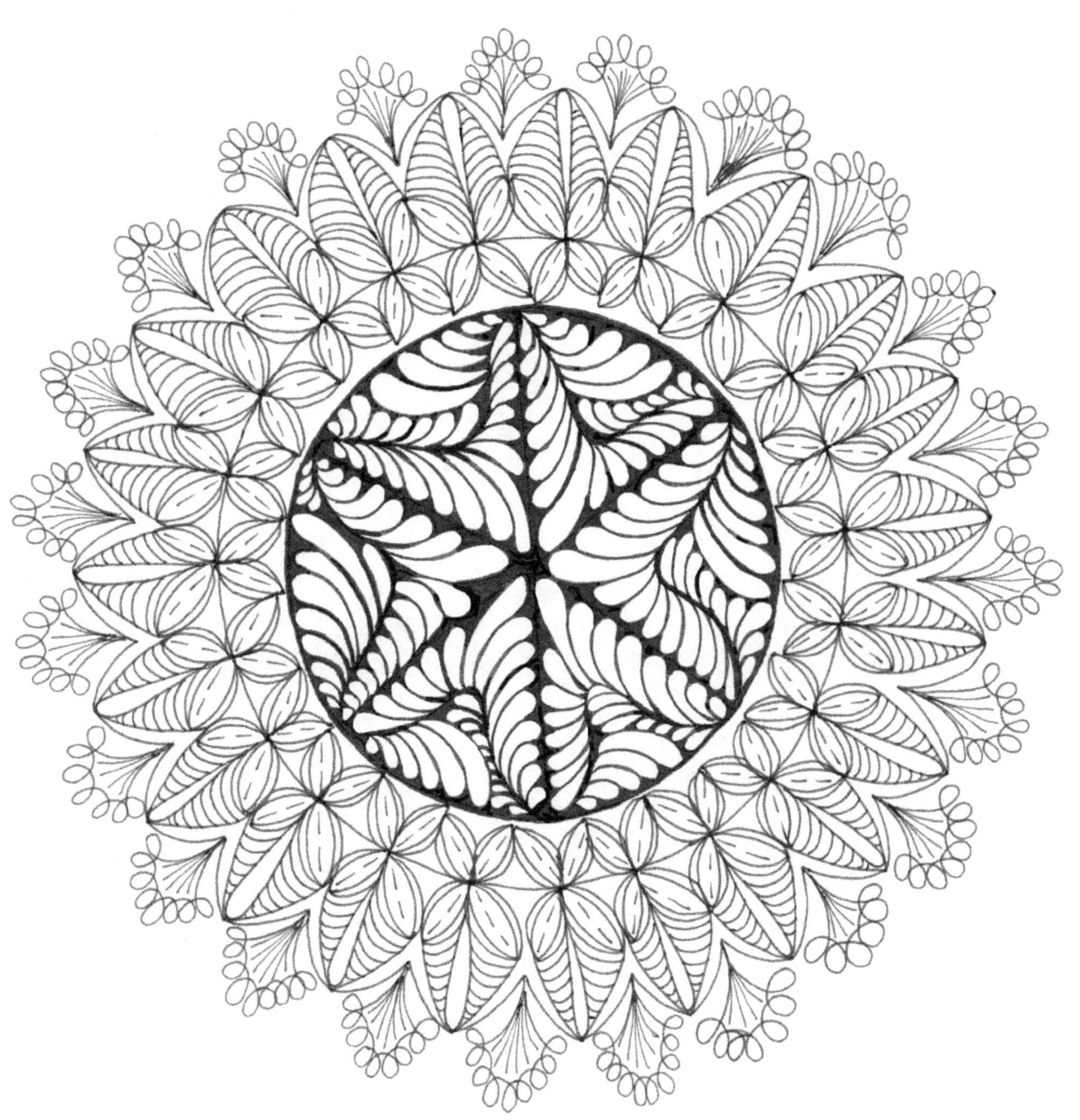

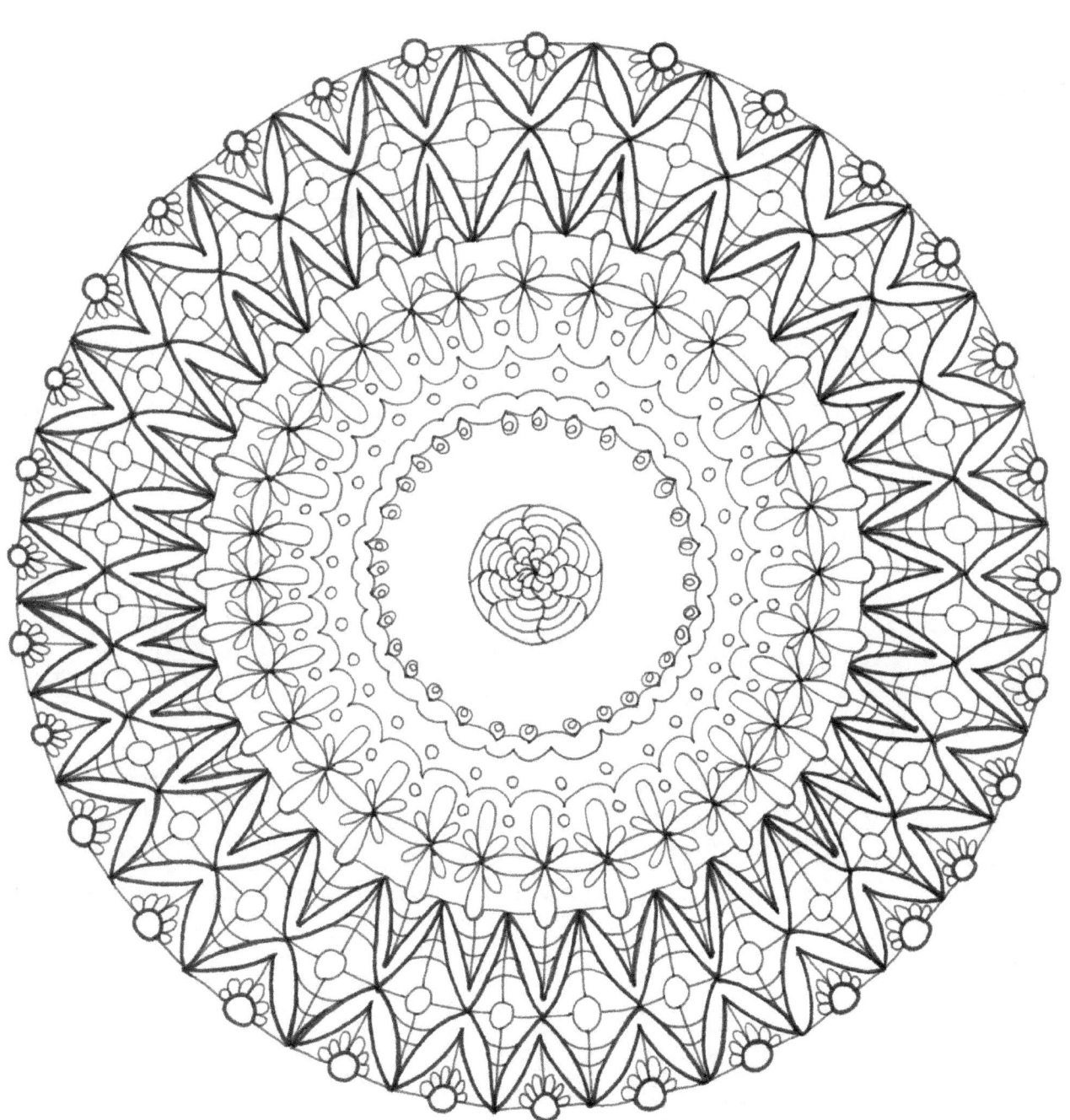

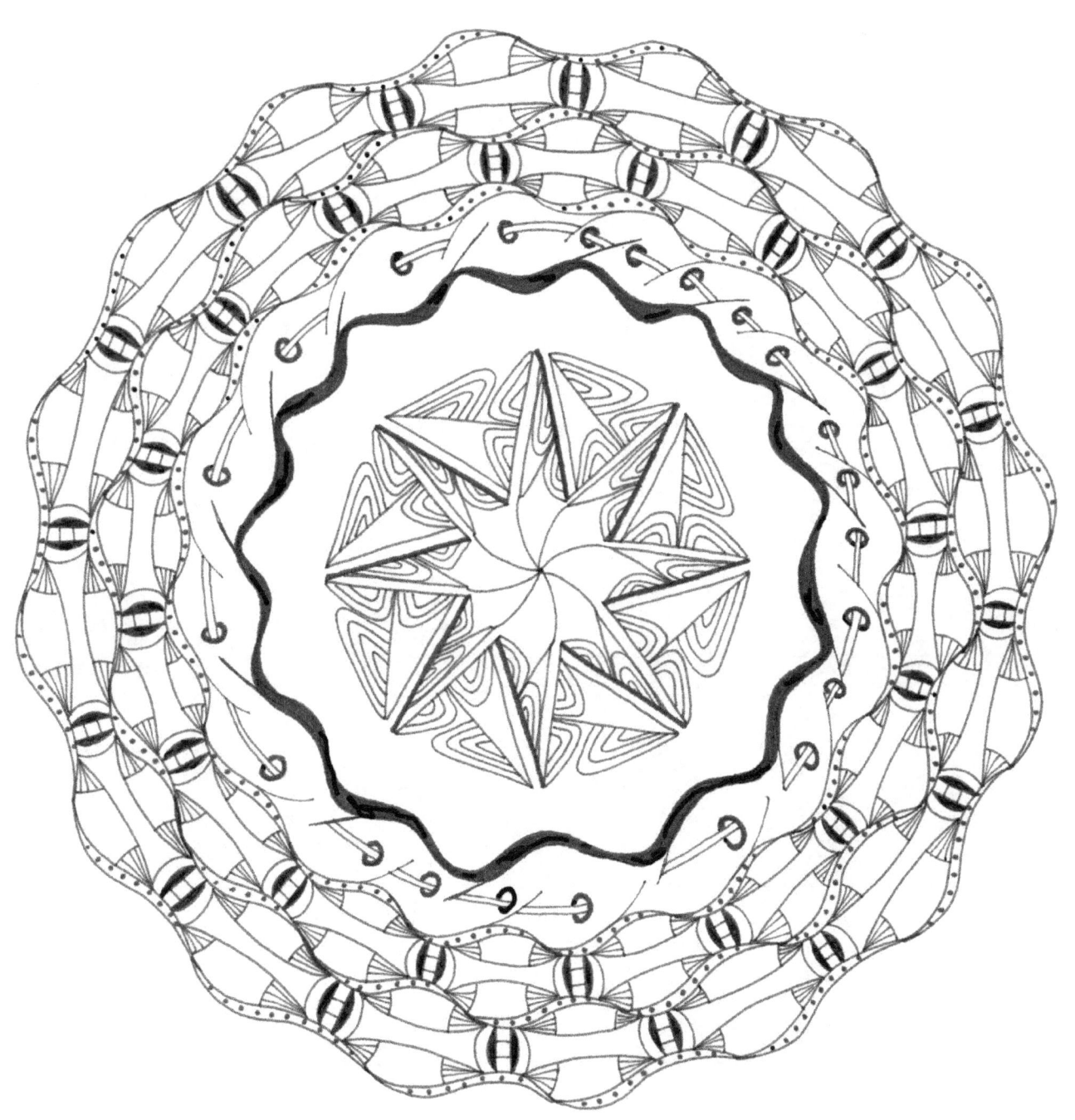

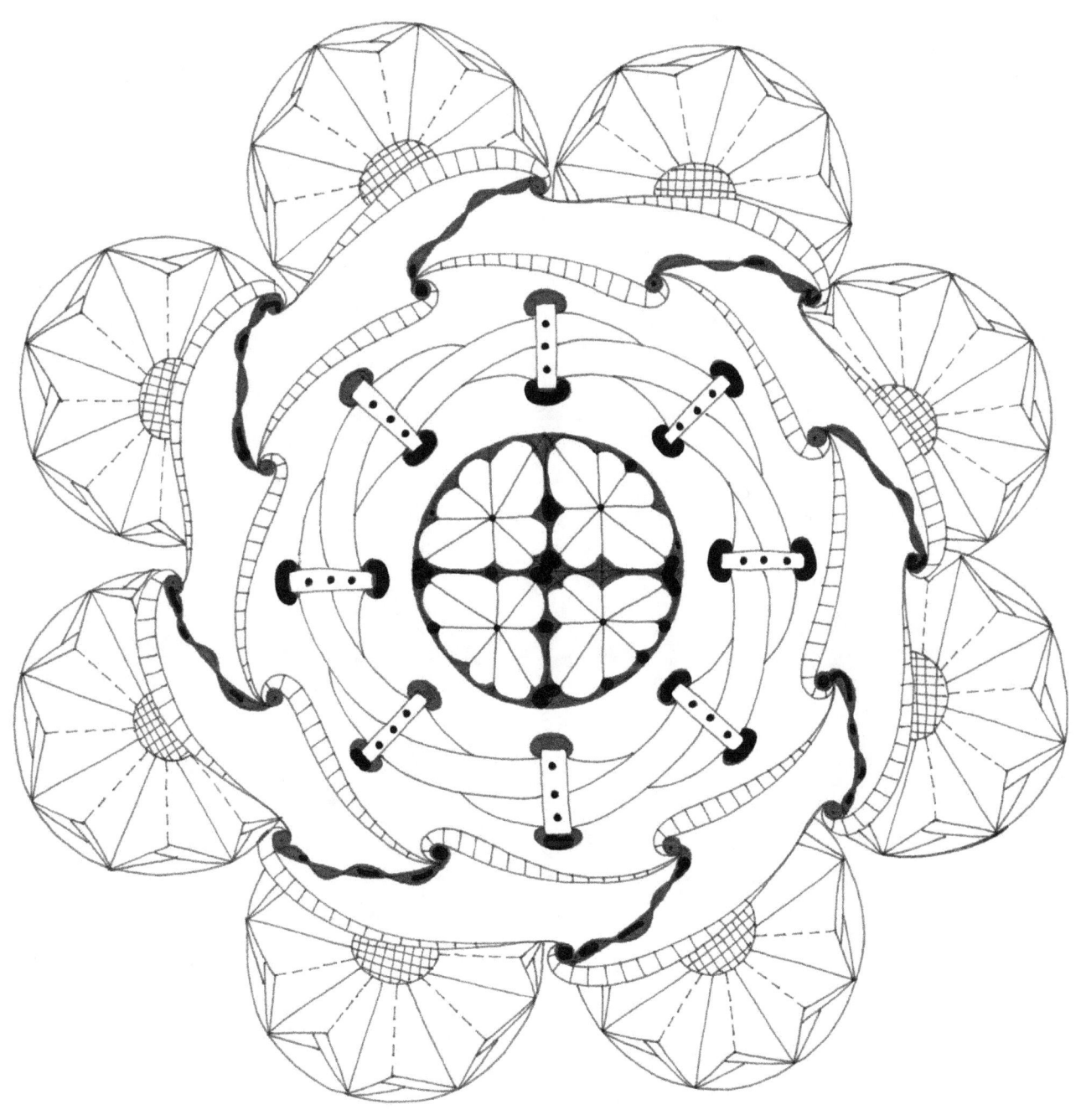

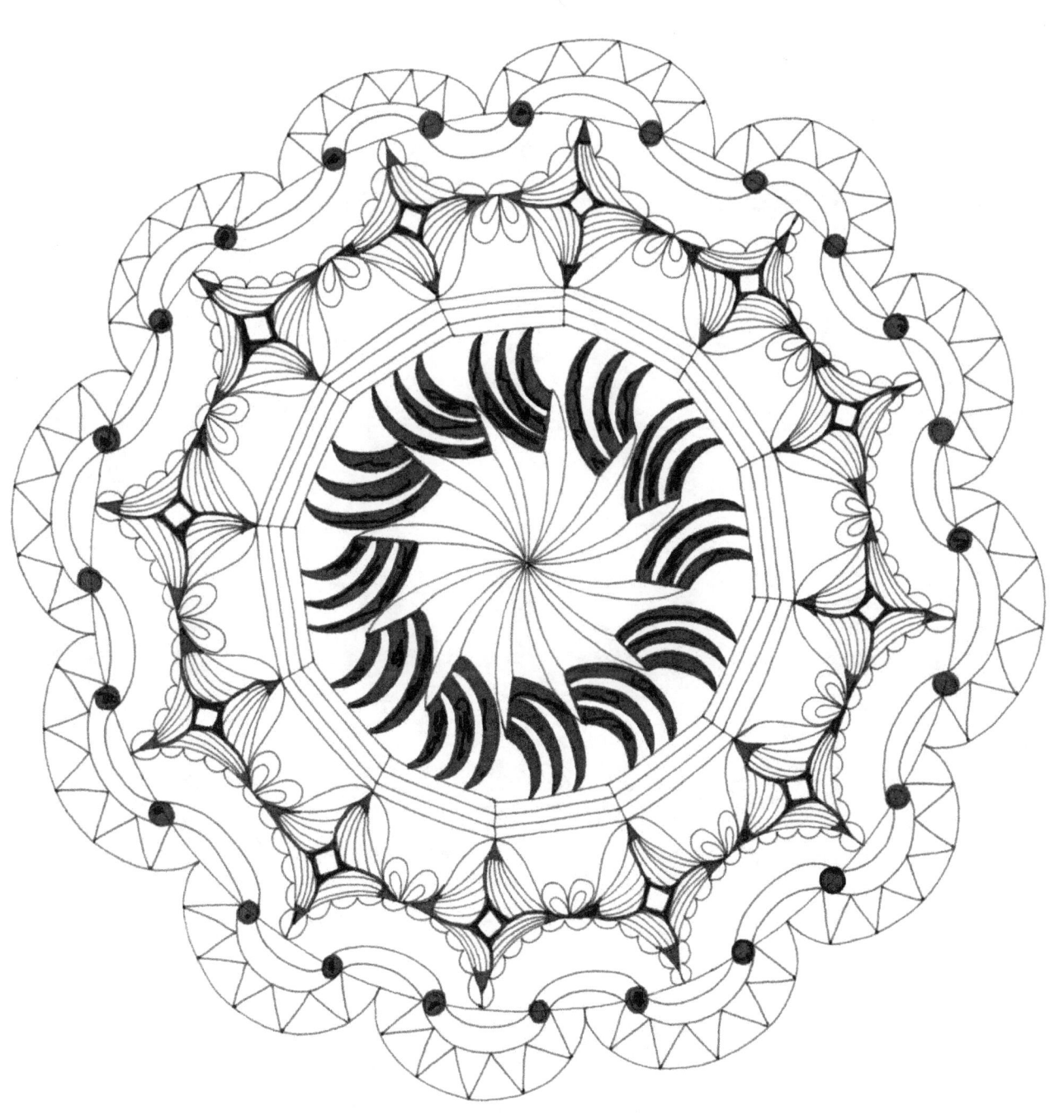

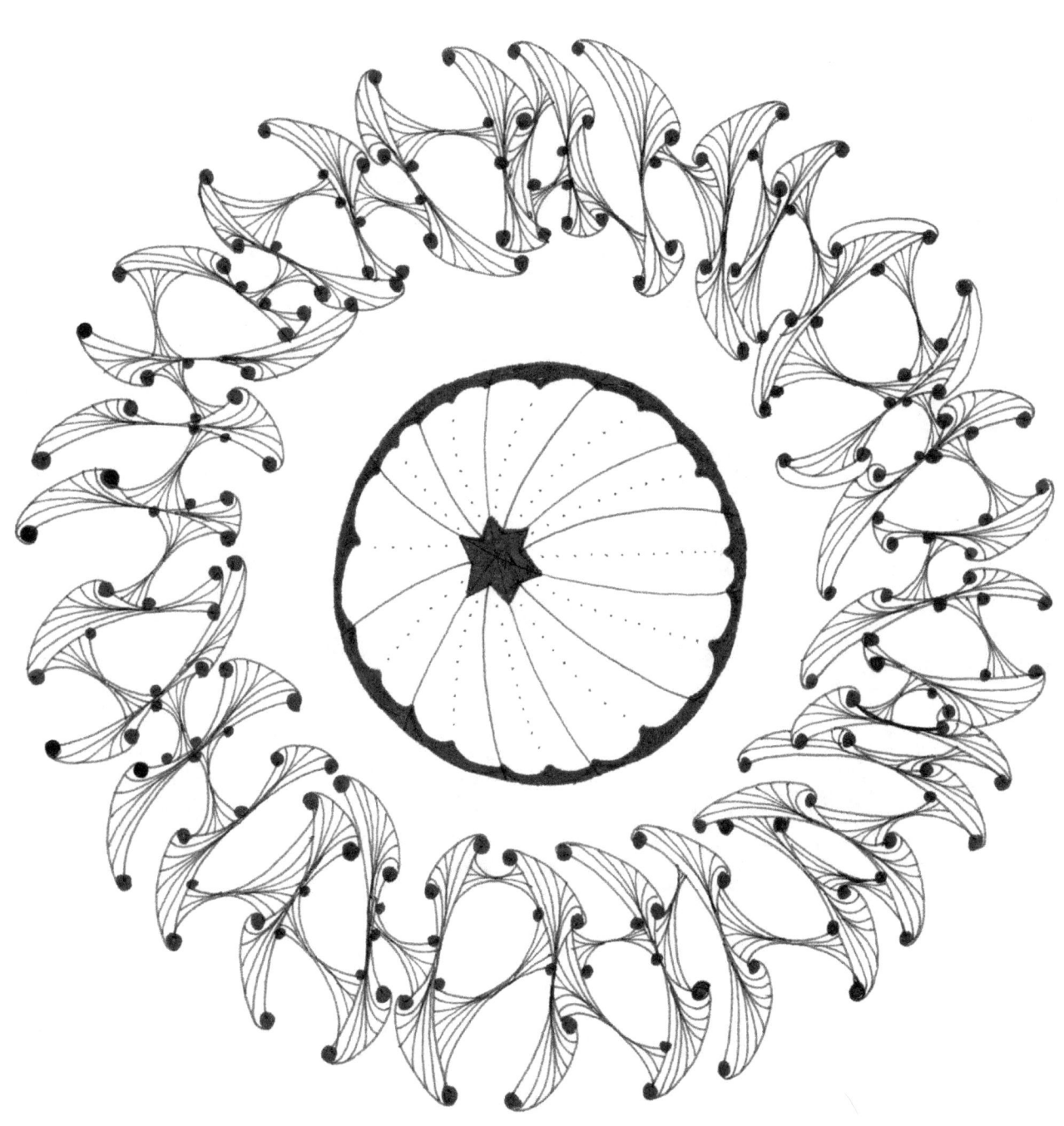

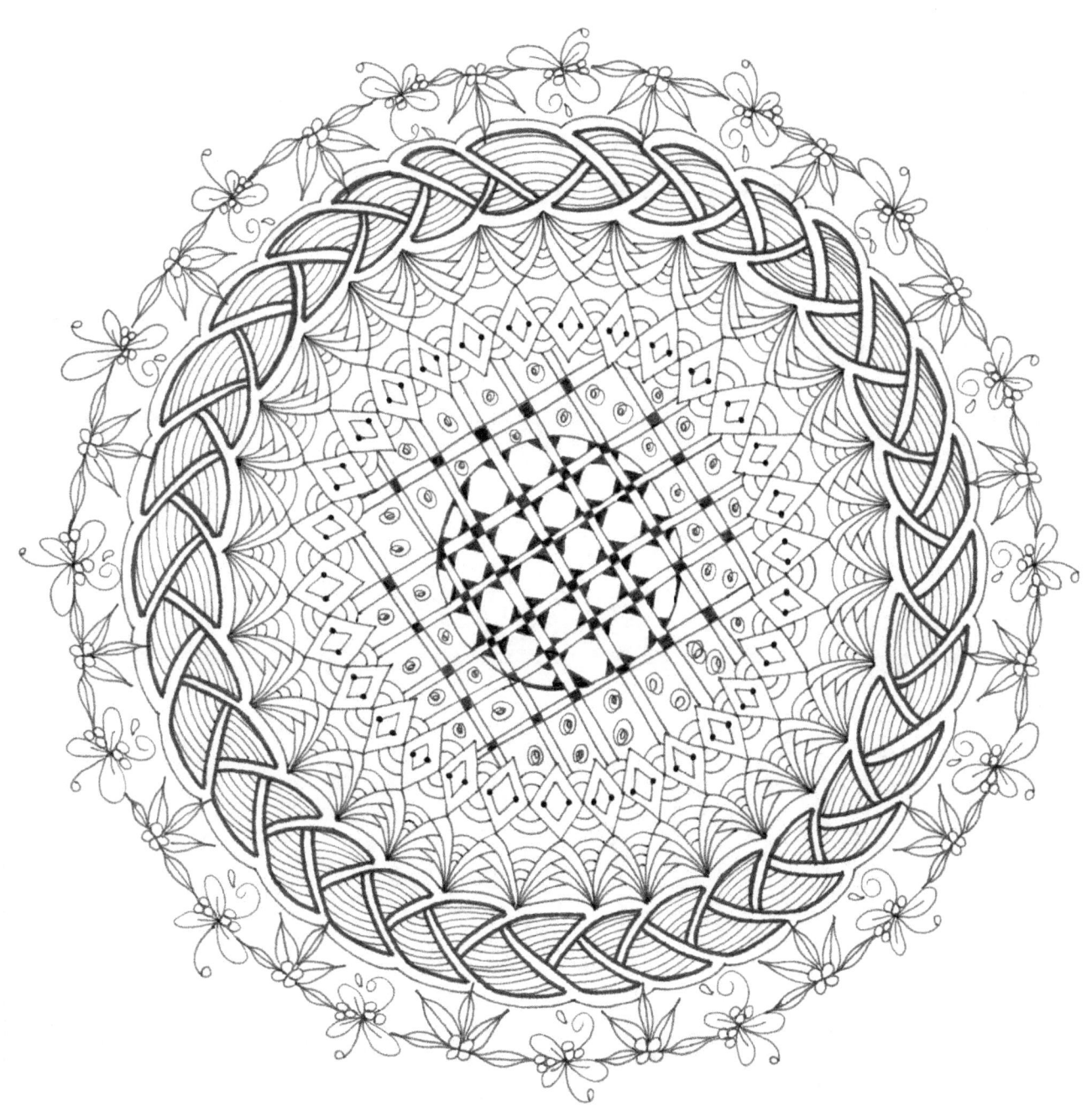

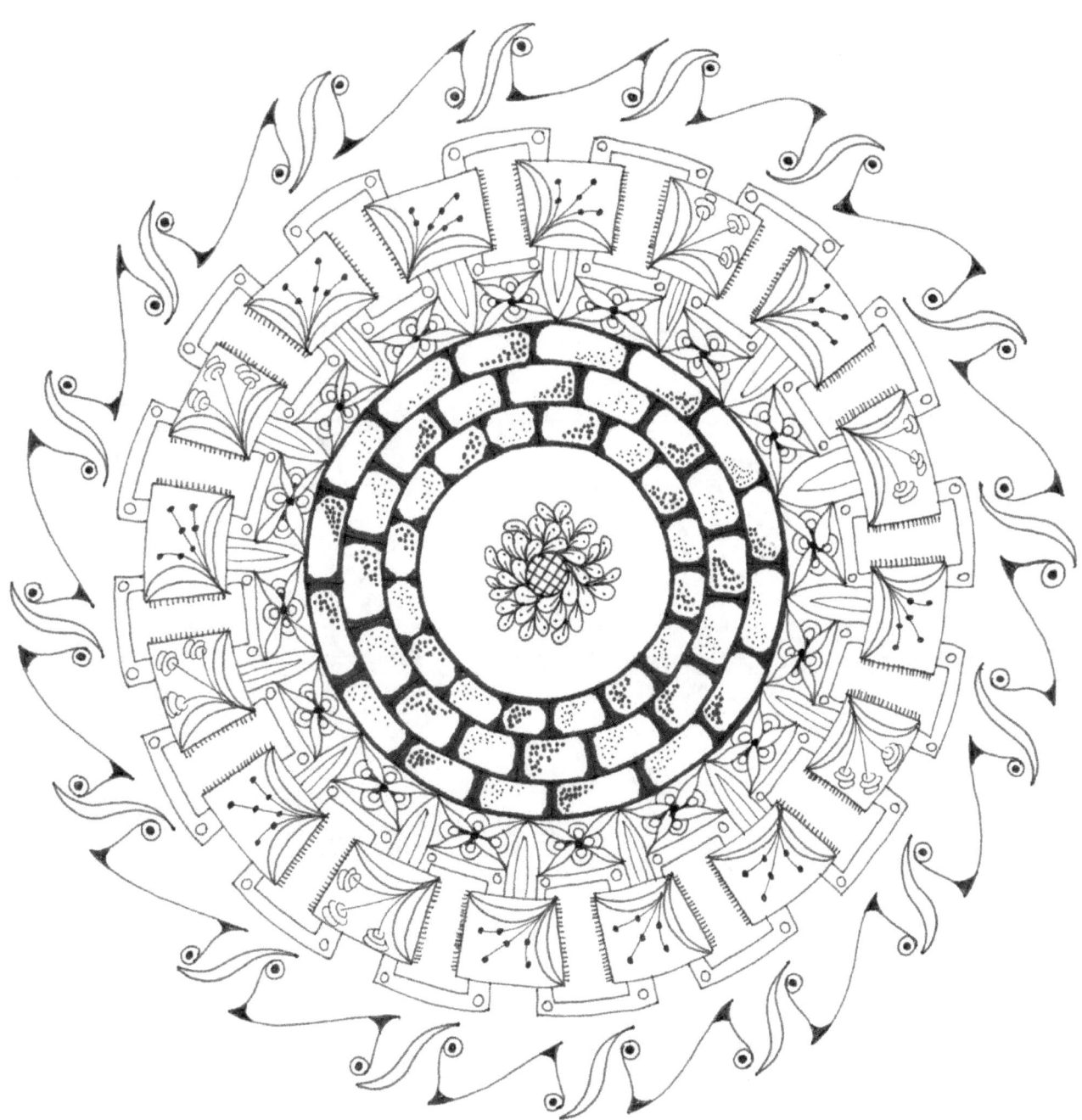

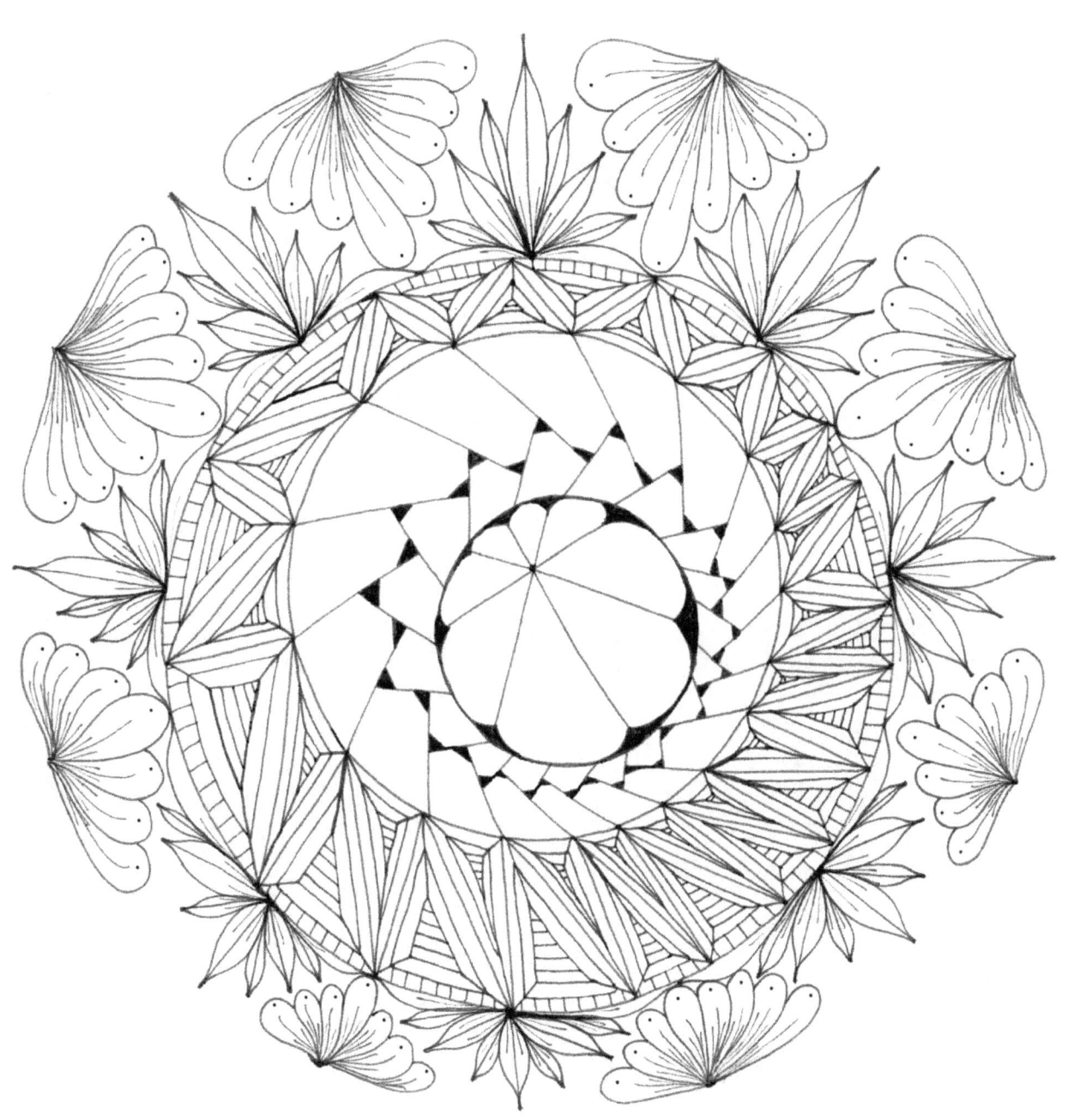

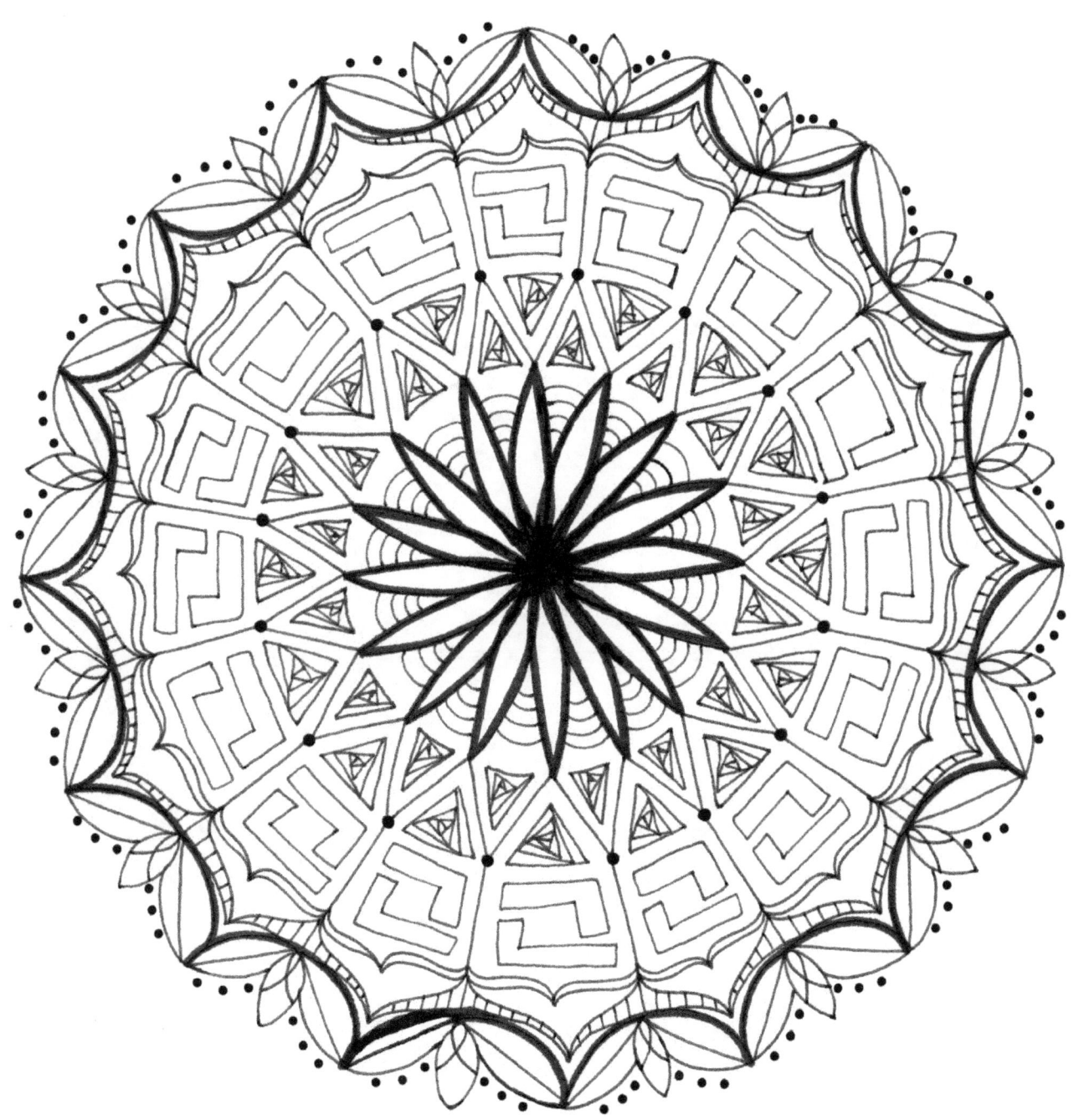

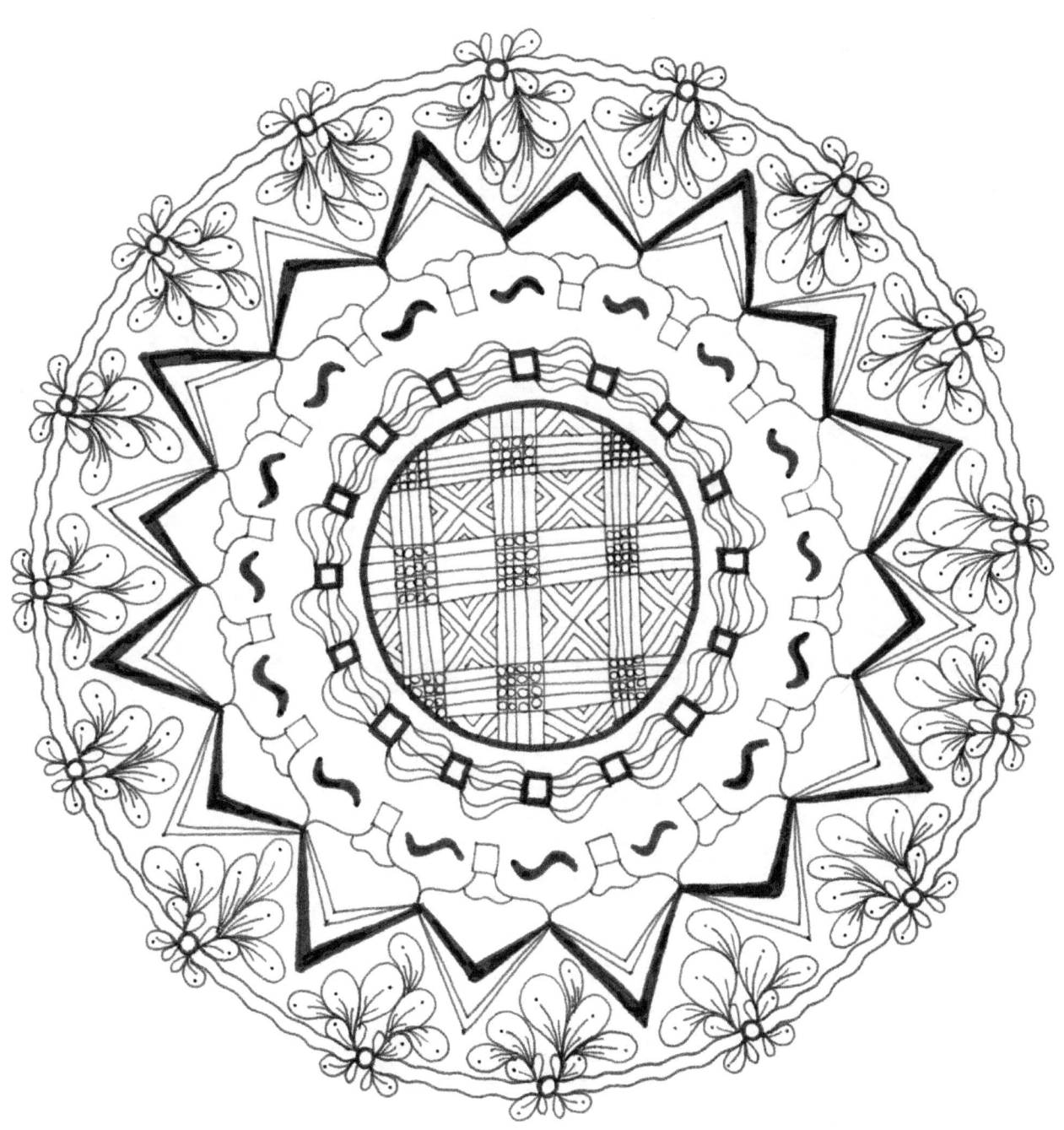

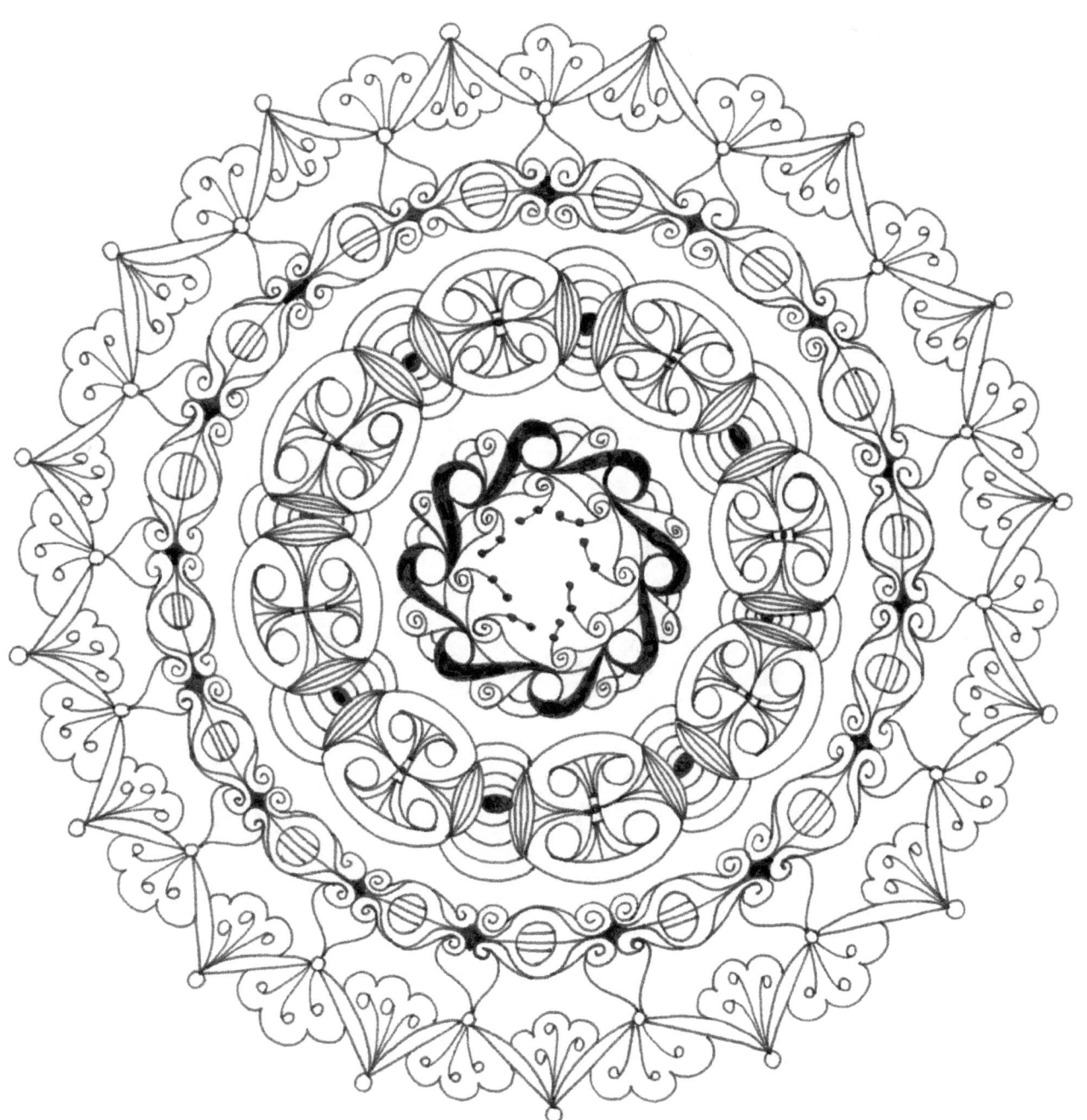

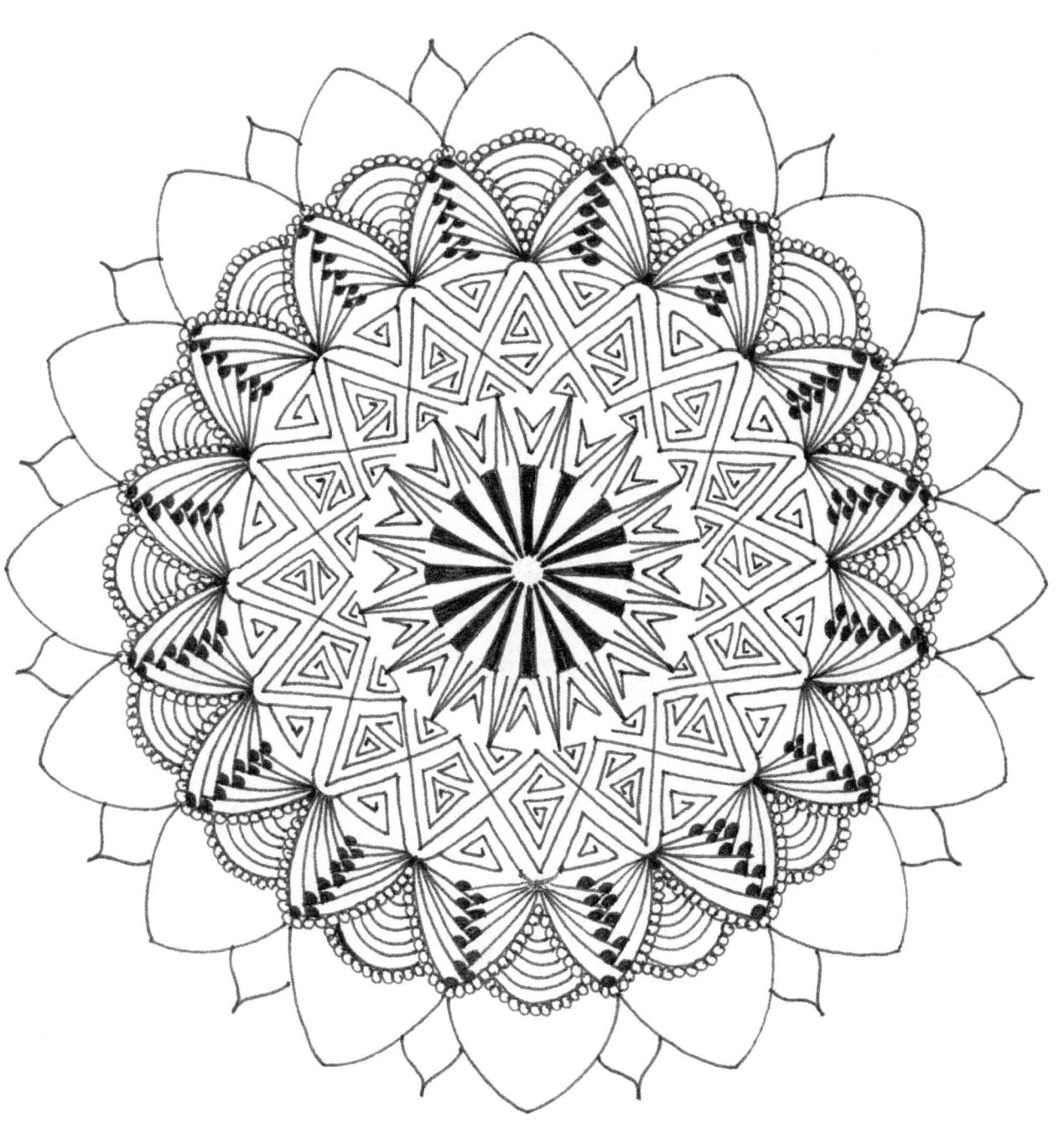

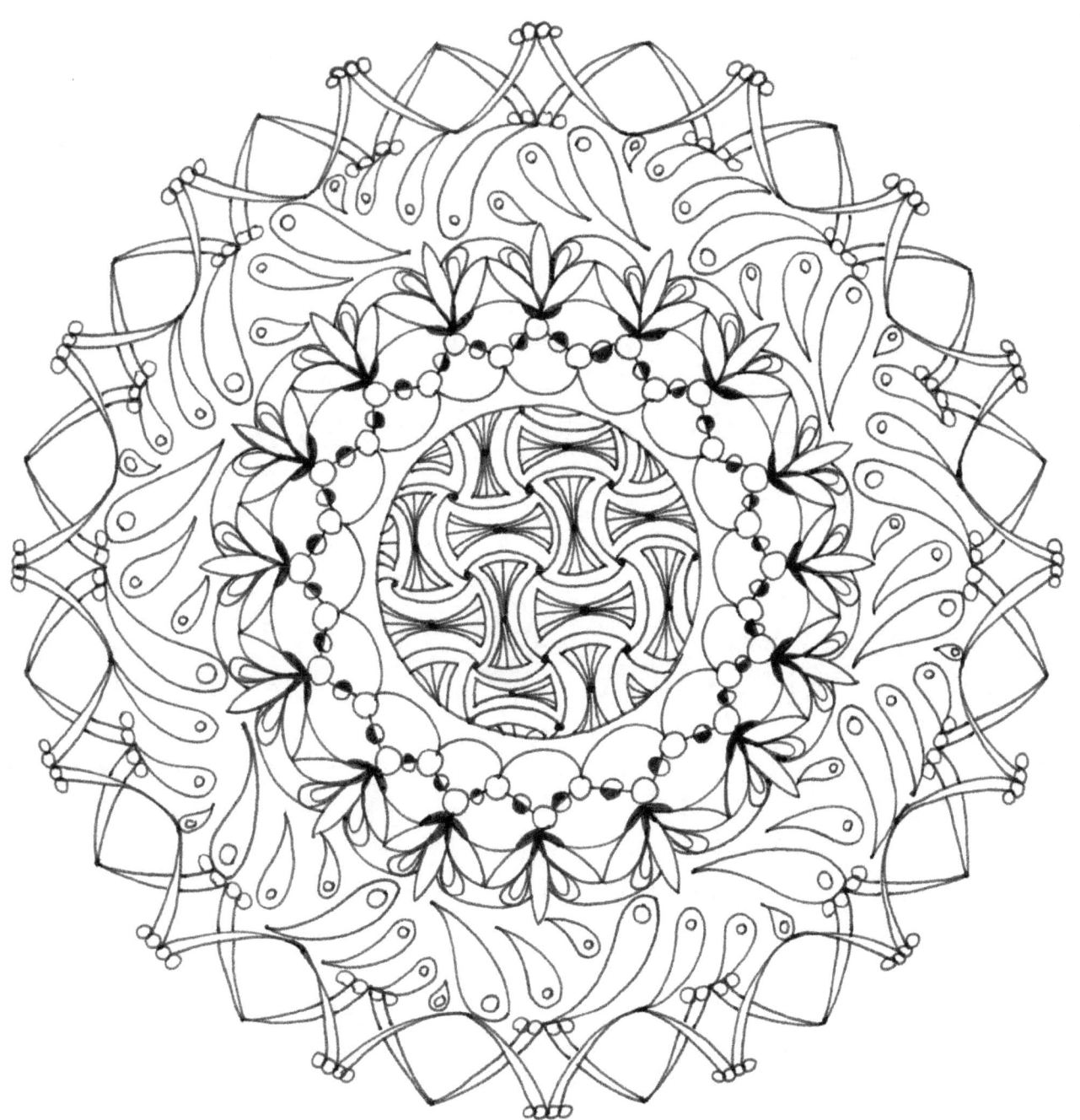

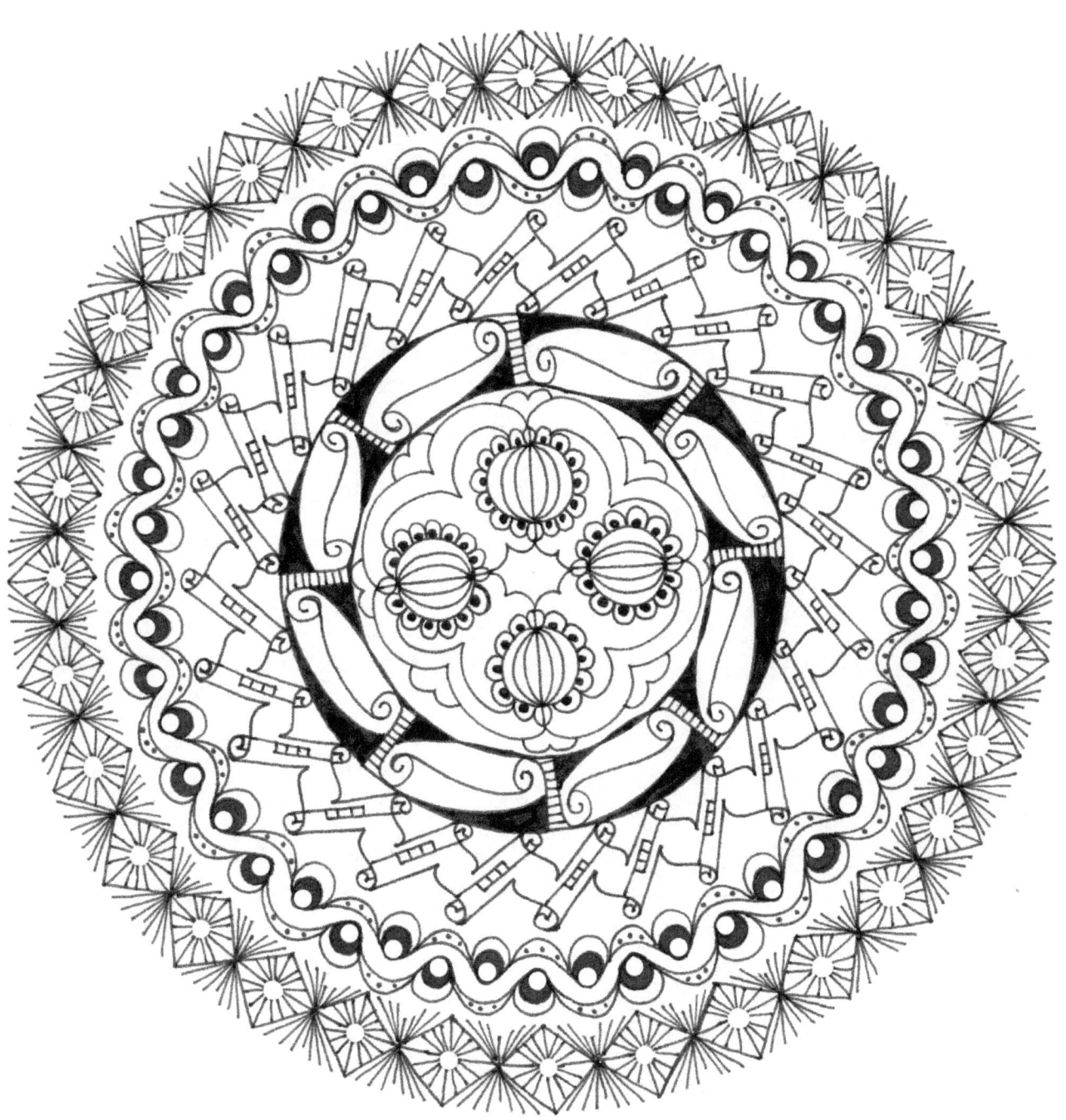

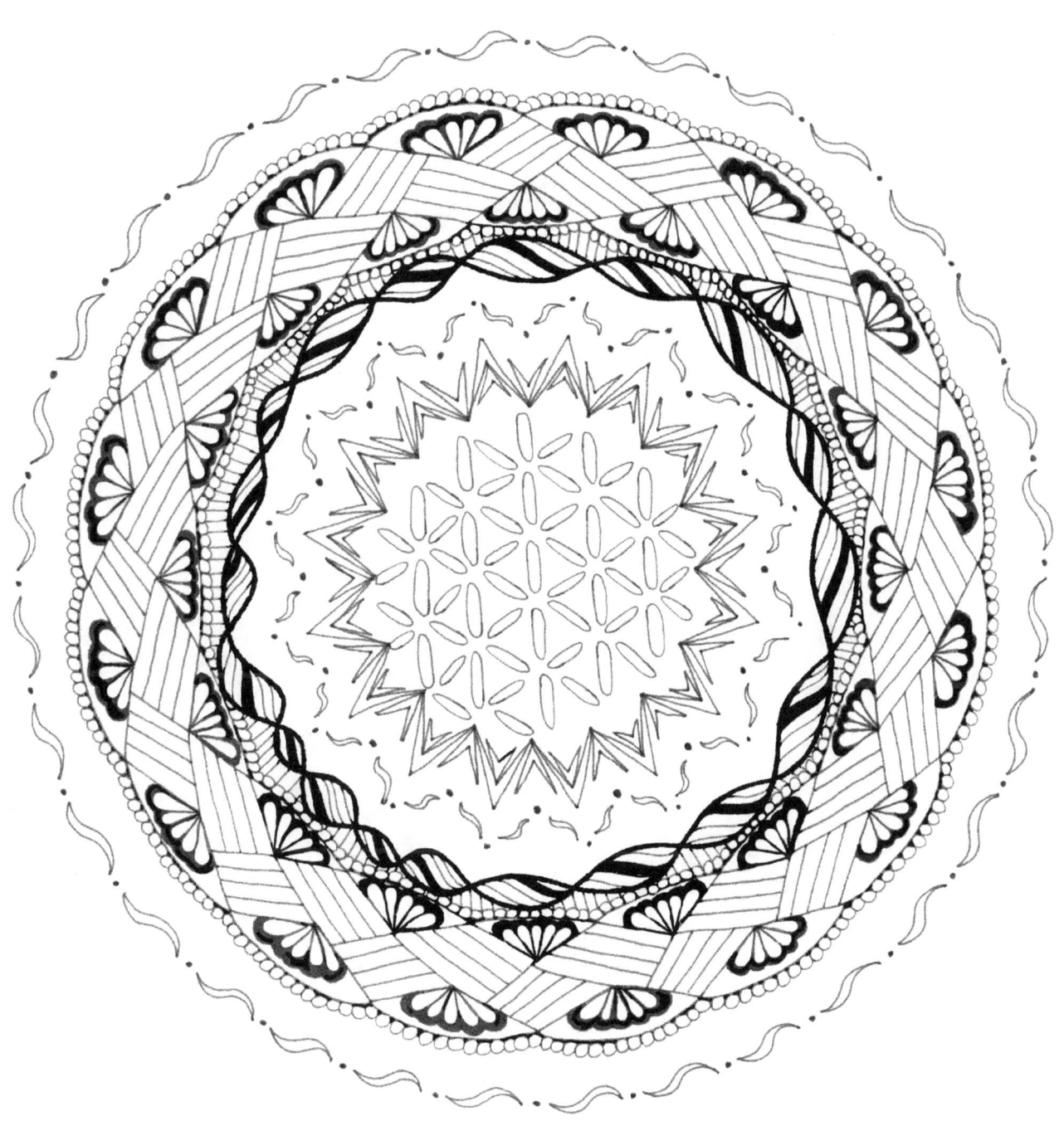

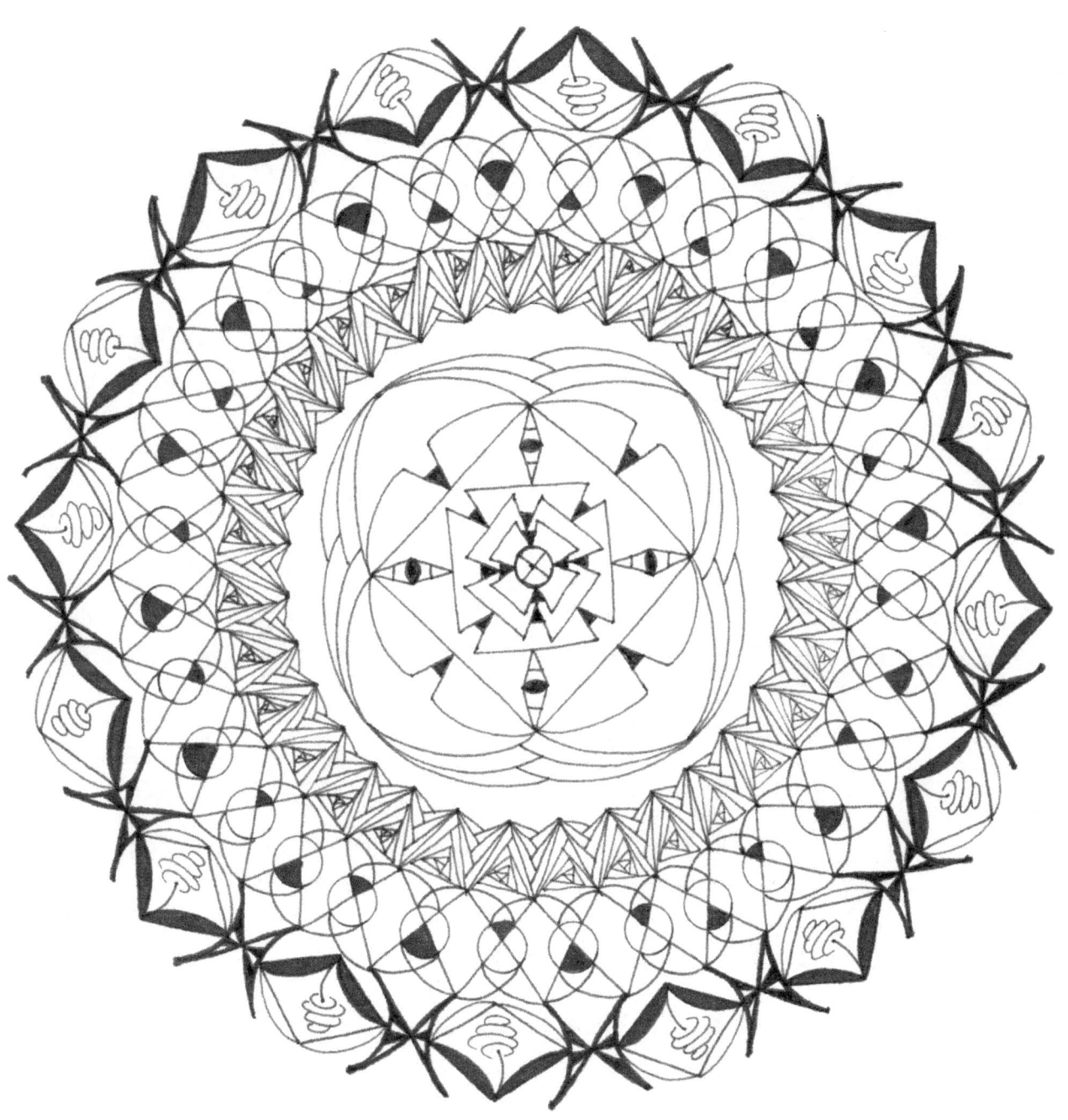

ABOUT THE AUTHOR

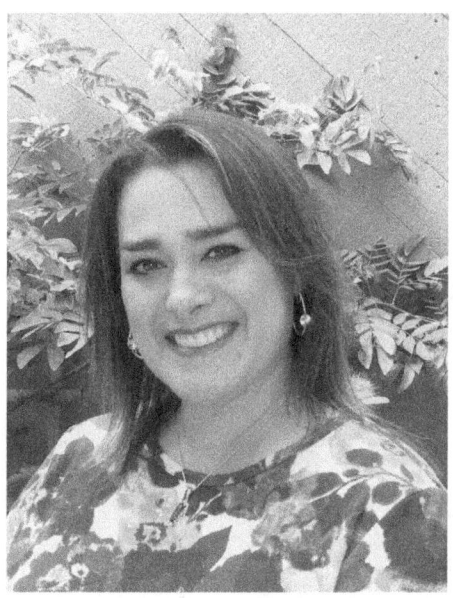

From the moment she first picked up her colored pencils and crayons, Theresa Beebe knew that coloring would change her life. With the huge void in her life from the loss of her job of 26 years and a very significant person, she was lost and unsure of what to do. Trying to put her life back together, she searched for ways to become more mindful and present to help recover from the debilitating grief. She started coloring. It's therapeutic qualities allowed her to relax and ease the tensions from daily worries and stress.

Theresa now offers the same opportunity to others through her own adult coloring books inspired by Zentangle. The designs and images she handcrafts are specially created to provoke a positive and meditative experience for anyone who chooses to color them. She hopes they bring as much joy to others as they have to her.

In addition to her artwork, Theresa is also a pianist. She was trained classically as a child and now enjoys playing new age.

Her advice to others is never give up on finding their passion. It's never too late as she's discovered at the age of 50. Theresa currently resides in California with her children. When she's not coloring or creating her own designs, you can find her listening to live music, playing the piano, hiking, enjoying the beach, and spending time with family and friends.

Theresa is currently working on her next book with several planned after that. You won't want to miss them!

If you have questions or want to contact to contact Theresa, you can e-mail her at mytangledjourney@gmail.com.

www.ingramcontent.com/pod-product-compliance
Lightning Source LLC
Chambersburg PA
CBHW080658190526
45169CB00006B/2172